WITH
A
LOVE

WITH
A
LOVE

To serve Christ is to live!
John 10:10b

Heather W. Johnson

by Heather Ware Johnson

WINEPRESS WP PUBLISHING

Sketches by Edward P. (Ted) Ware

Unless otherwise noted all scriptures are taken from
the Holy Bible, King James Version

ISBN 1-57921-277-8
Library of Congress Catalog Card Number: 99-69341

*Dedicated to all those who have prayed for
the Ware family throughout the years.*

CONTENTS

CONTENTS

FOREWORD

By Ted

This shall be written for the generation to come; and the people which shall be created shall praise the Lord. (Psalm 102:18)

O God, thou hast taught me from my youth: and hitherto have I declared Thy wondrous works. Now also when I am old and greyheaded, O God, forsake me not; until I have shewed Thy strength unto this generation, and Thy power to every one that is to come. (Psalm 71:17, 18)

By Milly

The story of our lives is written so that those who read it will realize that with God nothing is impossible (Luke 1:37). Ted and I put our lives in His hands for Him to use when we were fifteen, and sixty years later, we can write confidently of God's faithfulness. It is not what we have done, but what He has done. All that God needs is lives willing for Him to use. We pray that this book will bless and encourage you to let God have His way in your lives. You, too, will find it exciting and fulfilling to watch Him work.

Acknowledgements

By Heather

Isn't our dear Lord Jesus Christ wonderful! He cannot be praised highly enough. This book is a simple, true account of His ways and workings in the lives of some of His people.

I am Ted and Milly Ware's third child and oldest daughter. The accounts recorded in this book have affected me throughout my life and have instilled in me a deep love for God. He is real and is worthy of our entire devotion.

For many years, I believed that my father's story should be printed, and numerous people encouraged him to write a book. In 1992, he wrote down his early childhood memories, which became the basis for chapter one of this book.

It wasn't until 1994 that I started to see that it was not only my "father's" book. On one visit to our home, my mother explained some pictures that documented their first trip from England to the New World. As she spoke, my mother's bravery amazed me. I concluded that her perspective was necessary to do justice to the account. I found myself often thinking about what their book should be like.

One evening, my youngest brother, Paul, called me from his home in Washington state. "How's your Arizona weather?"

"Hot! And yours?"

"Wet."

To initiate a topic about which the newspaper did not already inform us, he asked, "What have you been thinking about lately?"

"Dad and Mom's book."

"How so?"

"Well, first, it isn't just Dad's story. Mom's thoughts and experiences must be part of it." I rambled on how I pictured it.

"Very interesting, Heather," he said. We said good-bye and hung up. Paul and I talk on the telephone three or four times a year, so I did not expect to hear from him for a while. Three hours later he called me again. "You won't believe this! After we talked, I went over to see Dad and Mom. Before I could get in their front door, Dad thrust a letter at me from Randy Larson, an English teacher from Wyoming. The letter said the exact words that you just told me. Call this man up!"

So I did. After initial introductions, I asked Randy, "What is the first step to write my parent's book?"

"Someone has to interview your parents and have them recount everything that they can remember onto cassette. They will think some of their experiences unimportant or uninteresting, but ask them to tell them anyway."

I thought I could handle that, so off I went to Seattle. I spent a week interviewing my parents and my brothers. My oldest brother, Kevin, astounded me with his recall, and I am grateful for his invaluable input. Twenty-four, ninety-minute cassettes of material later, I boarded the plane for home, confident that someone who knew how to write books would miraculously step out of the woodwork and write it.

When I got home I called Randy. "The material on those cassettes has to be put into a computer," he told me.

Our daughter, Gloria, had just finished a high school class in typing, so I asked her, "Would you be willing to type Grandpa's cassettes into our computer?"

"Sure, I would love to help!" Grandpa generously paid her for her efforts. When she was done, we had hundreds of pages of material.

I called Randy, "What now?"

"Someone has to go through the material, get rid of duplication, and organize it into time frames."

I thought, *Maybe I could do that.*

My husband bought me a new computer and printer to contribute to the effort. I embarked with the first finger on my right hand (the extent of my typing skills), and our youngest son, Micaiah's, endless patience to teach me how to use the complex computer. Hours, days, months went by.

Siobhan, our eldest son's wife, read ahead of me and helped to put the material into perspective. What an encouragement she was!

Dad wrote a beautiful song that is part of this book, made sketches to go along with the stories, and answered, along with Mom, my innumerable questions. A year later, the material was organized. I sent it off to Randy.

"This is good, but it still isn't a book. Someone has to make it flow. Someone has to make it live."

Hmmm, I thought, *I wonder how that's done?* Randy sent me ideas and wonderful examples that triggered my imagination. With every feeble effort that I made, Randy encouraged me as a father does his toddling infant.

One day I sat in front of the computer and thought, I will never learn to "walk." My typing finger is bruised, and the job is insurmountable. As I sat looking at the empty screen, the telephone rang. It was my mother.

"We just received a letter from May Godfrey and her sister, Neva Patterson. They are praying for you and the book."

A quiet confidence engulfed me. With their prayers, I knew I could do it. These two prayer warriors lived in the same city I did and allowed me to visit their home each week to read the latest chapter to them. I cannot put into words how much their love and support meant.

Our second son's wife, Bridget, encouraged me with her enthusiasm and laughter as she read the pages I had written.

Randy edited with such finesse that I never felt cut down or stupid as he corrected and improved the material I sent him.

After Randy, Dr. Virginia Allender, a lifelong friend of the family, corrected the material. What a privilege and learning experience it has been to work under such brilliant people.

Every prayer for the preparation of this book has made a difference. Thank you to each of you who contributed in this important way.

I desire to give special thanks to my precious husband, Lyle. Without his love, generosity, and patience, there would not be a book.

A thank you also goes to our children: Samuel, Josiah, Yehoyadah, Joel, Gloria, and Micaiah, for their love and support.

I am very grateful to my siblings: Kevin, Clive, Joy, and Paul, and their families, for their encouragement and backing.

Thank you for your important, individual contributions: Reynold Johnson, Tex and Vera Young, Carrie Menard, Kimarie Ware, Randy and Judy Larson, Von Vaughn, Loris Rolfe, Rudy and Kathy Bassman, Dr. Virginia Allender, and many others, whom God remembers.

As I look over the three and a half years that has brought my parents' book to this point, I am in awe of our wonderful Lord Jesus. "*With a love* that passes understanding," He has broadened my life and experience and has done exceedingly above all that I could ask or think.

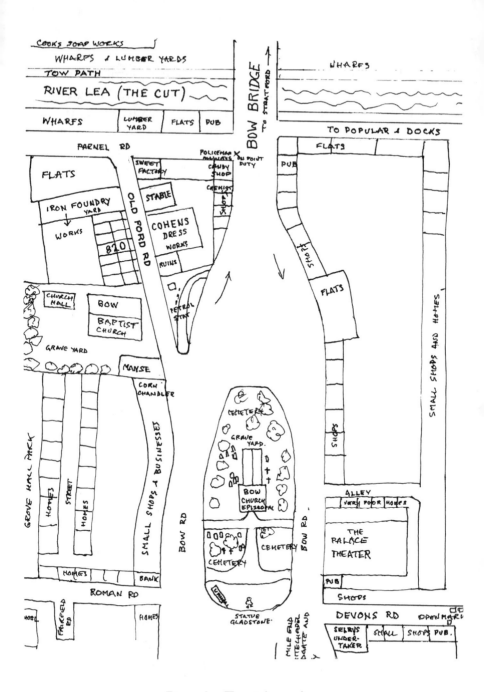

- Bow in East London -

The Streets of East London, 1920–1933

The yellow light from the gas lamppost danced upon us faintly through the shoe shop window. My friend, Tommy, and I yanked together at the last box of shoes left on the shelf. *Kerplunk!* A handsome pair of boots landed unceremoniously on the floor. Tommy put both his feet into one of the cavernous overshoes. The leather reached to his knees. With some difficulty, he stood up, balancing like a tightrope walker with outstretched arms. Tommy's father, a longtime acquaintance of my mother's family, owned this shoe store in Poplar, East London, over which both of our families lived and shared the tiny bathroom, kitchen, and meager laundry facilities. My family rented a room from Tommy's folks, where we stored our few possessions and slept. Tommy and I, both two years old, were our parents' firstborn and only children. Each evening after Tommy and I were put to bed, our parents went to the common kitchen and, drinking cups of tea, laughed and talked about the day. This evening, after a good night kiss, I went to sleep and dreamed of shoes.

"Eddie!" Tommy whispered loudly through the crack in the door. I awoke, jumped out of bed, tip-toed to the door, and worked at the big black knob. The latch finally gave, and the door creaked open. "Let's go try on a pair of shoes!"

That very afternoon, we had asked permission to do this, but our mothers said, "No, boys. The shoes might get scratched, and then they would have to be sold for less money."

"But we'll be very careful!"

Our mothers shooed us away, "Go and play together with the wooden blocks." The desire to cover our feet with strong new leather grew within us throughout the remainder of the afternoon.

When Tommy first knocked on our bedroom door, I rubbed my eyes to wake up. I thought I was dreaming. It wasn't until the longed-for aroma of leather surrounded us that I realized it was real. Tommy tried to hop in the boot that engulfed both feet. He lost his balance, grabbed for a chair, rocked precipitously for an instant, then crashed to the floor. We held our breath. The upstairs laughter stopped. I heard my mother. "Joe, is it a burglar?" The legs of four chairs scraped the floor, and I looked over at my mate's white face and big round eyes. The door opened. Tommy's dad appeared with a big stick from the fireplace, held like a club over his head. The other adults were close behind. As their eyes adjusted to the dimness, they saw us perched atop fifty pairs of new shoes. Tommy's mother gasped, "What a bad influence Eddie is on our Tommy!"

Father's strong arms scooped me up and whisked me from the scene. My gentle, brown-eyed mother followed closely as we hurried up the stairs to our room.

Soon after, my father found us another place to live. He borrowed a horse and cart, loaded all our earthly goods onto it, placed Mother and me on top, and slowly led the horse through the noisy streets of London to our new home: 820 Old Ford Road, in Bow.

As we meandered through the busy, dirty streets, my father chatted to cheer Mother up. She and her family had lived in Poplar as far back as she could remember. Even though our new home was only a few miles away, she felt like an uprooted begonia that hung with bare roots as she waited to see where she would be planted.

"You know, Flo," Father exclaimed enthusiastically, "it's a wonderful stroke of luck that I found this place! It has everything, and you'll be in charge of it!"

This perked Mother up a little. She had always waited in line for Tommy's mother to finish with the knife and cutting board before she could make my father a sandwich, followed by being told how thick to cut the bread and how much jam to use.

Father kept up his cheery conversation. "Bow is on the river Lea, a branch of the Thames River. A long time ago, the Old Roman Road met the river here. To get kings and people across the Lea, they built Bow Bridge, which is shaped just like the bow of a rainbow." My father pointed toward the arched bridge in the distance with a satisfied smile.

"After building it, the foundations slipped," Father continued, "which made it dangerous to use, so traffic was routed to the old ford upstream. That detour became Old Ford Road, where we're going to live!" My father had been reared in Bow and was proud to introduce us to it.

A breeze blew heavily in our direction. Mother pulled the edge of her dress up to her nose. "The smell is awful, Joe! Surely we won't smell that all day!"

"You'll get used to it," he assured her, and continued with more historical facts: "Sometimes the Lea is called 'The

Cut.' Do you see the towpath on either side of the water, Eddie? That's where horses pull barges loaded with goods to and from various parts of London."

The River Lea (The Cut) Towpath

"The water sure is dirty, isn't it, Daddy?"

"Yes. All the buildings along the river dump their waste into it," he said.

Our eyes watered as thick, rank fumes wrapped round us like a dirty blanket. "The smoke is coming from that building over there." My father pointed to a grimy brick structure that belched dark gray puffs.

"That's Cook's Soap Factory, and today's the day they boil the bones of dead horses to render the fat to make soap."

I thought about my weekly scrub in the bathtub and worriedly turned to my mother. "You don't wash me with horsey, do you, Mummy?" She drew me close and was just about to say something, when an enormous horse with a cart full of boxes pranced onto our side of the street.

"Heaven help us!" Mother screamed.

Father jerked our horse's reigns and shouted to the man behind the boxes, "Watch where you're going, matey! Sleep at home, not on the road." He turned to Mother with the explanation: "He must have been at the bottle last night."

At last, on Old Ford Road, my father stopped the horse. "We're here, Flo! We're here! Our own place!"

Mother clambered down from the cart. Sure enough, there was a door with the number 820 on it. Father worked the lock with a key. I sat on our possessions and watched my parents disappear into the doorway. Mother reappeared in a flurry and pulled me from the cart. "Come and look, Eddie, our own place!"

Our new home was two stories high, ten feet wide, and eighteen feet deep. There were two tiny bedrooms upstairs and a scullery downstairs, which contained a two-burner gas stove, a stone sink, a copper (a boiler under which a fire was lit to boil water for washing clothes), and a fireplace.

The Indispensable Copper

The small parlor just inside the front door had a gas meter in the corner. I stopped to look at it and asked my father how it worked. "We put pennies in this slot, Eddie, according to how much gas we use to light the house. Each week the gas man comes . . . and collects the pennies."

Father ushered us out to the back thirty feet of our premises. "There's even a backyard where you can play, and Mother can hang up the wash to dry!"

"Do you think we could have a dog back here, Daddy?" I asked, since I wouldn't have Tommy to play with any more.

As if he had already thought about it, my father said, "How about a little terrier? A mate at work is trying to find homes for a whole batch of them. I'm sure I can get you one."

Mother examined the outhouse, while I further questioned my father about the dog. "The outhouse is quite adequate, Joe, quite adequate," Mother said as she emerged from the tiny cubicle.

Just then we heard a loud bang! I jumped to my mother's side. Father quickly reassured us as he pointed across the back fence. "That's where they fix carriages. Don't be frightened. You'll hear it all of the time. It's the iron monger's shop."

A door slammed shut, and a scratchy voice quavered a tune from the direction of the side fence. We glanced up and watched a disheveled woman throw a pail of water out onto her back plot. She turned and saw us.

"Are you moving in?" she asked. "Because if you are, I'm telling you, the owner is a stickler for his money each week. He arrives Friday afternoon, exactly at two, dressed in his finery, with his gold pen and little book."

"Oh!" we said.

"And sometimes we have trouble in the water lines," she continued, "so the water man visits regularly; and don't forget to lock your front door each night. There's some undesirables about who might bother you when they're tipsy!"

Father put his arm around Mother and ushered her inside of our house. "Thank you for the advice!" he called back to the neighbor.

Soon our life took on a pleasant schedule. My father left each morning on the General Omnibus Company's red buses to work in London as a typewriter mechanic. He returned by 6:00 P.M., or earlier, if he was able to catch a green "Pirate bus" (a competitive, non-scheduled bus line that made better time). During the day, Mother hummed through her work in the house, and I either watched her or played. I was allowed the freedom of the backyard and the area immediately in front of our home. This gave me access to Cohen's Dress Factory, directly across the street. In warm weather, the factory doors were opened to let in any cooling breezes, and I would stand daily at this portal enchanted.

I watched rows of girls at sewing machines, deftly working bright pieces of cloth. A short buzz from a machine, a wisp of color, a flip of the material, another buzz from the machine. These girls glanced at me from time to time and flashed a smile. My heart skipped a beat. Often they sang

Cohen's Dress Factory

melancholy songs of the 1920's: *Carolina Moon* and *You Made Me Love You.* Then they would switch suddenly to bright two-steps and fox trots, their voices lifting gaily to the tunes of *Ain't She Sweet* and *Walking My Baby Back Home.*

Every so often the charge hand would come out to where I stood. "Off with you. Don't bother the girls!" He waved his skinny arms and scowled at me. I moved away, but hurried back at five-thirty in the evening, when the girls lined up to punch the clock. I had learned their names, and as they filed past, I murmured, "Good night, Peggy. Good night, Rose. Good night, Sue." On one occasion, Peggy stopped and gave me a quick hug. Her softness and warmth, her perfume, filled me with an insane delight. I worshipped her after that. The first woman I ever loved.

The first dog I ever loved, Father brought home in a typewriter box a few weeks after we moved in. Her name was Flossy, and she became my playmate. The first time that our "water man" met her, I was in the backyard. He had checked the pipes inside of the house to locate the trouble, then had come out to check the outhouse pipes. His head was inside of the small cubicle as he listened with his special stick to the mysterious gurgles in the lines. Just then Flossy ran up and snapped at his backside. The water man lurched forward, banged his head on the wall above the toilet, jabbing his eye with his water stick. Flossy kept barking as the man bellowed and swung his stick. Mother ran outside and grabbed me. "Eddie! Get in the house where it's safe." Then she rescued the water man from our barking Flossy.

Flossy always met us at the back door, tail wagging furiously, each time we entered her backyard domain. One day, Father left a pail of whitewash and a brush by the side of the back door where I couldn't miss it. My artistic mind went into full gear, just as she rushed up to lick me. She was black, and I wondered how she would look white.

Flossy stood at attention while I meticulously decorated her in a coat of gleaming whitewash.

Ten minutes later, I stepped back to appreciate my handiwork. Transformed, the dog stood robed in white as if ready to meet Saint Peter. Stiffly, she turned to lick her shiny coat and started to cough. This jolted me to reality. At any moment, my father or mother might find me! They possibly had another use for the whitewash, and just maybe, they wanted Flossy to wait for this heavenly robe!

Black Flossy Becomes White

Desperately, I tried to de-paint her with a towel that Mother had left on the clothesline. My mind raced with explanations. "I tripped over the bucket of white-wash, and somehow it landed on Flossy!" Or, "I walked into the back-yard and found her like this!"

Just then I heard my full name, "Edward Philip Ware!" I was doomed.

"Yes, Mummy?" I said sweetly as Mother approached.

"What are you doing?" She put her hands on her hips. Her eyes were dark and piercing.

"Helping Flossy. Somehow she got white-washed!"

"Be sure your sins will find you out, Edward! Clean her up!" My mother was not much on quoting Bible, but she regularly used Numbers 32:23 on me. Mother turned and went back in the house. I heard my parents laughing through the kitchen window, so I relaxed. But that night before I got into bed, Mother talked to me about Flossy and what I had done. "You tried all afternoon to clean Flossy, didn't you?"

"Yes, Mummy."

"She is going to look gray until her hair grows in black again. You tried to cover up your painting her, but things that we do wrong, and especially lies, have a way of wiggling to the surface like little worms in the dirt."

I knew about worms in the dirt, as I had dug up a plant in the park and quickly re-buried it, when one had crawled out of the hole I had made.

The next day was Sunday, and as I hurried home from afternoon Sunday school, my mouth watered at the thought of the tender roast beef, golden potatoes, and gravy-filled Yorkshire puddings that awaited me. But there was a dark side to this dinner: "greens," which I tried not to think about.

"How was Sunday school, Eddie?" Mother asked warmly as I hung up my cap and jacket.

"Great. They talked about Daniel in the lion's den."

"That's an exciting story. Hurry and wash your hands; your father is ready to eat."

I scurried to the table and sat at my place between my parents. My father tussled my hair. Mother brought in the hot food. She divided out the pieces of meat, potatoes, and savory puddings, finally ladling gravy into the Yorkshire pudding's steamy pockets. Last, she returned from the kitchen with a pan of olive-drab vegetables and plopped a healthy amount onto my plate.

"Do I have to have greens today?" I asked as I tried to keep the awful green juices from invading my potatoes. My stomach revolted and my appetite fled as the green river was absorbed by the white starch.

Some months previously, my parents had started to allow Flossy into the house. She hid under the table at mealtime. Whenever I thought I could get away with it, I offered the greens to Flossy. As much as I knew she loved me, I had never been able to coax her to help with them. On this particular day, I had the answer to my dilemma. My father was in a serious conversation with my mother about radio and how he wanted to make his own crystal set, so I thought I would not be seen when I scooped gravy onto the greens and lowered them to Flossy. She sniffed once, took a tentative lick, then turned away.

"Flossy!" I hissed under my breath as brown and green rivulets spilled onto Mother's clean linoleum floor from my clenched fist.

My father turned to me. "Is something the matter with Flossy?" I couldn't possibly get the green mass back onto my plate without being seen. "Eddie," Father continued, "what do you have in your hand?"

"I was just checking if Flossy wanted to get healthy!"

"Put your greens back onto your plate," Father said.

I obliged.

"Eat them up!" I wretched and heaved as I struggled to eat the vile vegetable. At last the mass went down. I gave Flossy a little kick as I enjoyed my Yorkshire pudding.

That night before going to bed I asked Mother, "Why do I have to eat greens when they remind me of the linoleum in the outhouse floor? They spoil the taste of Yorkshire pudding."

Jesus Tender Sheperd, Hear me

"Because your body needs them to grow strong. Not everything that is good for you is easy or tastes good, Eddie." She hugged me as I got down on my knees beside her, then we prayed for the sad, the hungry, and for the poor souls in hospitals.

I was with my parents in our happy home for another year, watching life in Bow go by our front door, when one day Mother said, "Eddie, you're four years old now. It's time for you to go to school."

After that, each morning I dressed in shorts (in those days you had to be fourteen to wear long pants), a jersey, and shoes, then hurried downstairs to a bowl of hot oatmeal or a slice of bread dipped in "dripping" (the tasty fat and juices from Sunday's roast). Afterward, I presented myself to my mother who carefully placed my school hat on my head.

"Be careful with your hat, Eddie. Not everyone can afford a hat with an emblem on it, and we can't afford to replace it!" Some children wore rags to school and odd hats with no emblems. Sometimes I wondered why I had a nice hat and most of my friends didn't.

For the first few years, Mother walked me over the wood-cobbled streets to school. Horses clip-clopped, hauling loads of freight; cars and buses beeped, carrying goods and passengers; bicycles and pedestrians sought the remaining space along with neighborhood children and barking dogs. Amidst this commotion, one morning a horse reared and broke from its harness.

"Runaway! Runaway!" people screamed.

We saw the horse's bulging eyes, flared nostrils, and sweat-drenched body, careen toward us. Mother turned white and grabbed me. She pulled me to the nearest wall and shielded me with her body. I could barely see what was going on, but I realized at that moment that she would give her life to save me. After the frantic animal raced past, Mother let go of me, and I watched a brave man run out and grab the desperate animal's bridle. He was dragged until he was able to gain the mastery of it and bring it to a stop. We all clapped. Our hero ignored the praise, but I noticed the happy gleam in his eye and his extended chest as he walked past.

Mother held my hand as we walked on to school. A hearse with a team of shiny black horses was coming down the street. The noble creatures pranced in unison with great, black ostrich plumes attached to their headgear. Black-suited, high-hatted grooms attended them as they carried the living and the dead on their last earthly journey together.

"Mummy, those horses aren't scary, are they?"

"No, dear, they are not. Whenever you see them come down the street, I want you to take your hat off and stand very still and respectful until they've passed." She removed my hat as we stood quietly together and watched the glass-sided hearse go by.

"Why are those people crying, Mummy?"

"Because someone in their family died, and they are going to miss them," she answered as she put my hat back on my head.

"Mummy, you and Daddy will never die, will you?" The thought had never crossed my mind, but paralyzed me now.

"Not for a long time, darling," she assured me as we entered the school grounds. Mother waved me away to play with my friends as she stopped to talk with some of the other ladies,

"Mornin', deary. Did you hear it last night?" Mrs. Leach, who lived on our street, greeted my mother.

"It was hard not to. Quite a row," Mother admitted.

"They say the Cooper woman was taken to the hospital," whispered the woman.

"No! How awful. She'll never come out," my mother said as if it was Mrs. Cooper's death sentence. The local hospital was avoided at all costs. However, when someone had the misfortune to darken that establishment's doors, they were considered to be at the mercy of whores and low-life sorts—the nurses.

"Yes, she's done in," prophesied Mrs. Leach with a shudder.

"How about their little girl?" Mother asked.

"I haven't heard. God help her! Hopefully it won't be the workhouse!" Mrs. Leach was envisioning that grim institution with bare walls and cold cement floors.

"It sure is a shame," agreed my mother.

Mrs. Cooper had often been the topic of conversation. She was a dejected little woman who lived in the "flats," the poorest tenement in the area. It was said that her husband beat her unmercifully. Sometimes Mrs. Cooper dropped her little girl off at school, but she never stopped to visit with the other mothers. When Mrs. Cooper passed them, the women fell silent until she was a few paces beyond them. Even though they were all desperately poor, the women still had a pathetic class distinction among themselves. They deferred to the woman whose husband was doing better than theirs and always talked about the plight of those doing worse.

Mr. Cooper, a huge *navee* (road worker) with leather straps around his calves was known for his uncontrolled strength when he was drunk. Neighborhood children got out of his way, after hearing about him from their parents. There was one person, however, who was never afraid of him, and that was his daughter, who daily flew to him like a bird, and was gathered tenderly into his tree-trunk-like arms.

My mother and our neighbor concluded the morning's gossip session, then started for home.

They had gone no more than a block, when Teacher ran toward them, waving her arms. "Come quick, Mrs. Ware! Eddie's put a pea up his nose, and I can't get it out!"

Mother forgot the neighbors and raced after Miss Jones to her son.

That morning, a friend had come to school with a peashooter, a six-inch tin tube from which he blew dried peas at various targets. He allowed me to hold some of his little missiles. Without thinking, I had inserted one of the little round peas into my nose. To my instant horror, I realized that it wouldn't come out!

"I have a pea stuck in my nose!" I cried.

My teacher tried to get me to blow my nose. Then she tried to reach the pea with her fingers, but it only went deeper. Mother and Teacher took turns pounding me on the back. A

31

few frantic minutes later, I sneezed, and the pea flew out. Mother returned home, and I went back to my seat.

After school, on the same day, contrary to strict orders, I let Flossy out the front door. She proceeded to chase horses. Mother had to run down the street after her. When my mother returned with Flossy in her arms, she was exasperated. "Eddie, I can't take this any longer. I'm going to run away and be a soldier, if your behavior doesn't improve!"

This produced marvelous results for a few days. I could not imagine life with Mother gone off to fight some distant battle.

Several months later, Mother went away for a week. I thought it was because of my misdeeds, and I was beside myself with anguish. When she returned, she carried a squirmy bundle in her arms. She called it my "brother."

Five years passed before Mother delivered Joan in our upstairs bedroom. Cliff and I were shushed and shoved around downstairs. After what seemed an eternity, we were invited upstairs to meet our little sister.

Mother no longer walked me to school, but she always asked about my day when I got home. "What was your favorite class today, Eddie?"

"Oh, Mum! I drew the most wonderful picture of a boat out on the ocean. The art teacher told me it was very good. He said that it was even better than the steam train I drew yesterday. "

"I'd like to see it! And how was the math lesson?"

"Oh, all right, I guess." I quickly changed the subject. "My friend George told me today that they got 'electric' light in their house. Are we going to get it?"

"Actually, yes. This very afternoon!"

Later, a man arrived from the Fixed Price Electric Light Company. He ran a single wire into our house and installed a light in the living room. To our amazement, when we pulled on the cord that hung beside the bulb, a bright, magical light appeared.

"Coo, it's like the middle of the day!" my father said that night after work.

We each pulled the string until Father ordered, "Now, now, we don't want to break it before we've had it one evening. There'll be no more pulling tonight!" We reluctantly stopped the exercise, but marveled all evening over the instant, glorious light that modern science had provided.

Each evening, under the new light, Mother, Cliff, and I played games at one end of the dining table, while my father worked on projects and his hobbies at the other. Sometimes he brought a typewriter home to repair.

"Daddy, why do you work all of the time? Wouldn't you like to play with us?" I asked.

"I'm working for an aspidistra plant, Eddie."

"A what?"

"Every home worth anything has an aspidistra plant in the front window, doesn't it, Flo?"

"Well, yes," Mother confessed.

Not many months later, Mother had her very own plant placed carefully on a stand by the window in the parlor. It wasn't the most beautiful plant I had ever seen, but there was something to be said about rising in the world.

I thought again about the differences I saw between my father, who stayed home at night, and my friends' fathers who always were at the pub. Also, most of my friends' homes did not have an aspidistra plant.

The Glorious Aspidistra

"Daddy, Jeffrey told me that he plays an interesting game with cards every night with his parents. Why don't we have cards?"

"Because cards are associated with fortune telling, gambling, and drinking," my father said, "and those things cause a lot of trouble and sadness."

"Yesterday I saw Mrs. Jones beg her husband for money for food for their children, right out on the street! Then Mr. Jones threw back his arm and hit her, and she fell down. It looked like she went to sleep on the ground!"

"Listen, Eddie, you're eight years old now, and I need to tell you a few things. Mr. Jones drinks alcohol and spends nearly all of his money on it. When he has liquor inside of him, it takes over, and he doesn't act like himself. He's actually a really nice man. Your grandfather drank and gambled when I was a little boy. On his payday, he would stop to gamble before he got home, so although he had a good job with the railroad, he rarely came home with enough money to feed us. My mother had to go out to work. She was a kitchen maid in a hotel, worked sixteen-hour days, and made just enough to keep us from starving. While she was gone, we children were left at home with a neighbor who did not care if we had shoes on our feet in the snow. One of my brothers died of pneumonia after he caught a bad cold."

My father was nearly in tears. "Each night my mother had me kneel beside her and say my prayers. One night I asked God to make my daddy a good daddy. While my eyes were closed, I heard someone crying. I looked up and saw your grandfather in the doorway. Shortly after that, he started to go to church and made things right with God. He no longer gambled or drank, and my mother had a better life."

I was surprised to hear this about my grandfather, since I often visited my grandparents on the weekends and walked with them to church.

One Saturday, Grandfather and I walked to the chemist's (pharmacy) together. On the way, we passed a group of dejected, miserable men who carried signs as they marched past us. "Who are they?" I asked as I turned to watch them go on down the street.

"They are miners out of work, Eddie. England is in a depression, so there are a lot of problems. These men have no way to feed their families." I felt terrible for them and added them to the list of those that Mother and I prayed for every night.

Another day, my grandparents came to our house and asked my mother, "We've heard that the king is going to go by Mile End Road this afternoon. Would you mind if we took Eddie with us to see him?"

I was excited to go, so my mother put on my best clothes, and my grandparents handed me a little Union Jack (British) flag to carry and wave.

When we arrived at the street, there was a multitude of people, all with flags. Grandfather put me on his neck, but all I could see were flags and lots of people. Then I caught sight of the royal carriage. It stopped not far from us, and King George greeted one of our neighbors! How we wished it had been us!

Another famous visitor came to our poor neighborhood one day, Ghandi of India. He was in London to try to gain freedom for his country from the Commonwealth. Mr. Ghandi was housed on Pommes Road, because he insisted to stay where the poor lived. This was just around the corner from Grandmother Ware, so she took me to see him.

I was frightened at his unusual appearance: dark skin with a cloth wrapped loosely around him, round glasses, and a little mustache. There were many children around him, and I murmured "hello" to him. He smiled.

As Grandmother and I walked home I asked her, "Why is he so thin?"

"Well, Eddie," she explained, "he's a man who loves his people and sometimes doesn't eat to bring attention to their needs. He practices what he preaches, he does." She looked down at me tenderly. "It's amazing, Eddie, what one man can do in this world." I thought, *If a little, practically naked man like that can do something in this world for others, maybe I could too.*

Ghandi, always ready to talk to children

Once, while I was at my grandparents', my Uncle Jack, Father's brother, asked me, "How would you like to learn to play the trumpet? If you want, I'll teach you. Then you can go out on Sundays with us."

The Berger Hall Free Methodist Church in Poplar was associated with Guiness, the brewery master, who supplied money and silver musical instruments to the poor east Londoners. This made it possible for us to learn an instrument. Since the brewery was the cause of the vast majority of the heartaches in our neighborhood, I guess its owners slept better if they made some attempt at restitution.

At eleven years of age, I joined my uncle in the band. We practiced all week. Then on Sunday morning went out on the streets, marched to a given location, formed a circle, and played Christian music. Our leader, a man with wavy, white hair, often preached from Matthew 11: 28: "Come unto me, all ye that labour and are heavy laden, and I will give you rest". Certainly his audience could identify with the words, but only a few looked out of their doorways and listened to him tell about Jesus' love for them. At the end of his talk, we lined up again and played as we marched back to the church.

Another church that I was involved with was Bow Baptist, two doors from our home. I attended every function that they had for my age: Cubs, Christian Endeavor, and the Sunday afternoon Sunday schools.

Each week my parents gave me two pence to put into the offering at Sunday school. With the coins in my pocket, I felt like a man of means. I hurried past the church door and entered the local convenience store, where I bought a piece of candy with one pence. My conscience bothered me, but the sweetness in my mouth drowned anything it had to say. I was taught at Sunday school that Jesus had been little like me, so I hoped he understood our splitting the money.

In church I learned Bible stories and Christian songs. Each year the Sunday school put on a Christmas party. Awards were always good books. I received *Pilgrim's Progress*, *The Cloister and the Hearth*, and many other classics. These whetted my appetite to read, so I started to frequent the library; autobiographies, poetry, and adventure stories were my favorites. The Sunday school also treated us once a year to an adventure into the countryside or to some large park for a picnic.

The only other time our family left Bow was for a week in the summer. We traveled on the London Northeastern Railway to Southend-on-Sea, a twenty-five-minute train trip to the shore, where we splashed in the sea and cavorted on the pebbled beach.

Of course, my father had a few days off at Christmas, but we always stayed at home, and relatives came to see us. On Christmas day, the Wares came over. Our parlor, only used at Christmas time, was festooned with bright paper chains we had made. All through the day, the adults sat and reminisced. They interspersed tales with gales of laughter. Sometimes they lowered their voices and told stories that were "not for young ears." I sat very quietly with my young ears turned in the opposite direction and pretended to be busy. Thus I learned all kinds of interesting things. Later in the evening, Uncle Jack led us all in the game of "Follow the Leader." We sang and jostled around as we copied his every antic. If he stepped over a chair, we stepped over it. If he did a turn in the middle of the room, we all did. The game created a great deal of merriment.

Mother's family, the Sucklings, visited us on Boxing Day, the day after Christmas. Mother's forebears were seamen and shipbuilders who believed that they could trace their lineage back to Lord Nelson. I don't know about Lord Nelson, but I could sure see Long John Silver of *Treasure Island* fame in my grandfather as he stomped around the house on his wooden leg, which had been removed due to sugar diabetes. He always wore a seaman's jacket, open at the chest, no matter the weather. Known to drink a quart of whiskey a day, he also gambled. When Nanny Suckling died, my grandfather Suckling came to live with us for several years. I loved him and his stories of ships and the ocean.

Both he and my father smoked delightful "S" shaped pipes. As I watched them from day to day, I longed to indulge in this manly act. Jeffrey, a good friend of mine from school, agreed with me.

Our Father's Pipes

At the opportune moment, we borrowed our fathers' pipes and huddled together in the corner of an alley several streets away. After we lighted up, great puffs of gray smoke billowed from our mouths. After a little practice, we felt like men. Unknown to us, an unsympathetic woman who saw our smoke reported to my mother. I was met back at home with, "Be sure your sins will find you out, Eddie!"

Following that episode, Jeffrey and I raided the local park and brought armloads of stolen flowers to our girl-friends.

For Our Girls

When Mother discovered our theft, she sent me to the iron monger's for a cane. These devices were imported from some heathen country for the castigation of small boys. The salesman never questioned my purchase, but let me sort through the canes to choose whichever one I wanted. These whips averaged three feet long and were very willowy. At school, I had experienced the use of this implement when I was whacked on my hand two or three different times. I bought the cane that I believed would issue the least pain, then worked it back and forth all the way home, in order to take some of the sting out of it. When I gave it to Mother, she promptly issued my punishment.

One autumn afternoon, a school pal and I walked through the local park with our catapults (slingshots). We targeted various plants and trees. Then one of us accidentally hit a window in the park keeper's house. Stunned at the power of our weapons, we aimed at the other panes too, until there was not one window left. I slept fitfully for days, waiting for the park keeper to find me. He never did.

It was the exception, rather than the rule, when I escaped getting caught. At twelve years of age, it was my Sunday morning duty to get up and bring my parents a cup of tea in bed. To me, this task was a nuisance, except for the biscuit or cookie I could snitch while I worked in the kitchen. However, one Sunday morning, I was especially irritable. I knew the rules for making English tea: first the teapot must be heated by rinsing with boiling water. Then with utmost precision, one teaspoon of tea per cup of tea is measured, with one extra teaspoonful "for the pot." This brew is steeped for three minutes. That morning, such an exercise seemed entirely unnecessary. I poured boiled water into the cold teapot, took the lid off of the tea can, and dumped into the teapot what I considered the right amount of tea. Confidently, I sallied up the stairs and presented the tray to my sleepy parents.

"Thanks, Eddie," Mother muttered as she brushed wisps of hair from her eyes. She then pulled herself up and sat against the headboard. I balanced the tray on her blanket-covered lap. Automatically, she poured two cups of tea, added the necessary teaspoon of sugar, and dollop of milk.

I watched as she closed her eyes, raised the cup to her lips, and took a swallow. Immediately, I knew I had a problem. Her eyes opened wider than I had ever seen them before, and she started to gag. Father awoke instantly and began to bang Mum on the back.

41

"Paint, Eddie! It tastes like paint!" she wheezed. "Go get more milk!"

I nearly fell over myself as I raced downstairs, then back up again with the bottle of milk. No matter how much milk, sugar, or extra water was added, the tea remained tea-paint.

"Eddie," Mother told me, "you will have to give account at some time for all of your actions; your sins will always find you out."

Often, when I arrived home late from school, I found it hard to explain to Mother that I had stood on London Bridge for those missing minutes and watched as the water flowed out to sea. I daydreamed of stowing away on one of the many ships and sailing across the ocean to wondrous adventures.

Other times I was late due to travel escapades on land. My school buddies and I jumped onto the back of horse carts or lorry (truck) tailgates for a free ride home. The horse cart drivers, infuriated, lashed back at us with their whips.

"Get Off My Cart!"

42

The whips never quite reached us, so we held tight as the vehicle got up speed. We were often carried farther than we wanted to go, so we'd walk a long way back.

One afternoon, after telling Mother that I was late due to a delay at school, there appeared at our front door an unhappy policeman. I stood behind Mother.

"Madam, is your son Edward Ware?"

When I heard my name, I almost wet my pants.

"Yes, he is!" Mother said with a worried look on her face.

"Well, madam, he has been observed jumping onto the back of moving vehicles. This is an illegal act, madam. Further, the last time he was nearly run over by a truck. Nearly killed, madam."

The report was grossly exaggerated in my opinion, which was worth mud at that moment. The policeman continued, "I warn you, madam, he'll end up in Borstal, if he isn't watched and kept from such foolishness."

We both gasped at the thought of me in reform school. My mother was nearly in tears. "Yes, Officer. We will deal with him, Officer. Thank you." As she closed the door, the "bobby" frowned at me and turned away.

"Your sins have found you out, Eddie." Mother started to sob. "Go to your room and wait for your father." Still crying when my father got home, she told him of my criminal activity.

"Edward, your adventuresome spirit has gotten you into trouble," my father said as he spanked me with his shaving strap. "It isn't that you should never do exciting things, but you must consider the dangers, and your mother's feelings."

On another occasion that I "did not consider the dangers," my father destroyed a go-cart that I had painstakingly built. "You would get run over by a car in that."

I was frustrated that he could invent and explore new technologies, but I couldn't. When crystal radio sets came along, he built one. I sat beside him for hours, intrigued with the coils, knobs, and valves. Our whole family marveled at the sounds of music and voice that issued from the earphones that he had put together.

I remember vividly the day a horse-drawn van drew up to our door. The driver proceeded to unload typewriter after broken typewriter into our home. These were stacked against the walls, under the beds, and on the stair steps. Every spare inch of the house held boxes of parts. A typewriter repair company had liquidated and sold my father its entire stock. I heard my parents talking the night before.

Thousands of Typewriters

"Flo, it's an incredible opportunity! If we buy these typewriters, I can fix them and then sell them."

"Yes, Joe, but it will take everything we've saved."

"I know. But it's the only way we will ever be able to get enough money to move to a neighborhood that is better for our children. We will never be able to rise in the world just on my salary."

"Whatever you think is best, Joe," Mother said.

Every night I watched my father work on typewriters. Each day he took a fixed machine into London and sold it. One typewriter was dreadfully warped. "That one looks too bad to fix," I said as Father studied the damaged machine.

"It had a nasty fall off a desk, I think, Eddie," he said as he continued to survey it. Then to my utter amazement, he raised it about two feet off of the ground and dropped it! When he retrieved it, behold, it worked! After he had cleverly noted the direction in which the frame was bent, he banged it back in the opposite direction.

The money saved from my father's extra labors grew, until one day he came home very excited.

"I've found us a new place, Flo! We're moving!"

THE HILLS OF KENT, 1919–1933

"Daddy, do the flowers and the trees belong to Mr. Gordon-Brown?" I asked from my perch on my father's shoulders as I surveyed nature's bluebell bounty all along the tree-lined lane.

"Yes, I guess you might say they do," he replied as he adjusted his collar.

"Daddy, do the cows eating grass over there belong to Mr. Gordon-Brown?" I could see one mother cow carefully licking her soft brown calf with her big tongue.

"Yes, Milly," he said, and started to sing a favorite hymn.

"Daddy, please," I interrupted, "what about the birds singing? Do they belong to Mr. Gordon-Brown?"

"Yes," he said after a pause, "the birds are nesting on trees on his property, so you could say that they are his."

"And, Daddy, what about our house?"

"Yes, that too belongs to the Gordon-Brown estate."

A pause, then what was really on my mind. "Daddy, I live in one of his houses, so whom do I belong to?"

"Milly, you are Daddy's own precious little girl," he assured me.

I patted his neatly combed brown hair. "Daddy, do you belong to Mr. Gordon-Brown?"

He stopped and looked out over the fields. "No, I work for him, but I belong to God." He gave my braids a tug and started to sing again. We continued for another mile without questions.

As the country village came into view, I could see the silhouette of the tall Church of England steeple. "Daddy," I asked, "what are you going to talk to the people about this afternoon?"

"Well, my little Milly, I want to make sure that everyone knows that the Lord is coming back very soon."

Mother always said that she thought that Daddy was in a rut on this subject, but he must have liked being in a rut, since I never heard him deviate from it.

He proceeded to quote 1 Corinthians 15:52: "In a moment, in the twinkling of an eye, at the last trump: for the trumpet shall sound, and the dead shall be raised incorruptible."

I batted my eyes to see how quickly a "twinkling" could be as we entered the village with its humble cottages and pleasant flower-strewn front yards, passed the stone arch of the Church of England, and headed to the little chapel a few blocks beyond.

"Good evening, Mr. Halliday," a bowed old man greeted my father. "I see you've brought a rose from your garden with you."

My father was the gardener on Mr. Gordon-Brown's huge estate, but I knew that the old man meant me. I blushed as I squeezed Daddy's neck with my legs.

Inside the church I sat quietly on the front bench. After a few hymns, Daddy started to speak.

"I would like everyone to turn to Matthew 24:37 and 40. 'As the days of Noah were, so shall also the coming of the

Lord be. Then shall two be in the field; the one shall be taken, and the other left.' Now, please, look up Luke 17: 30 to 36. 'In that night there shall be two men in one bed; the one shall be taken, and the other shall be left. . . . Two men shall be in the field; the one shall be taken, and the other left.'"

Daddy continued talking, but the terrible word "left" had stuck in my mind. Surely, if Daddy went somewhere, he'd take me with him, especially if he went so far away as Heaven!

I thought about this through the rest of the service, then fell asleep on the pew. The next thing I knew, I was being tucked into bed next to my sister, Ruth.

"Good night, Daddy. Don't go anywhere without me." I murmured as I fell back to sleep.

In the morning, I ran downstairs, gulped my breakfast, helped Mummy clear the table, then asked, "May I please go and help Daddy today?"

"Yes, Milly, your sisters, Gladys, Grace, Elsie and Ruth can help me in the house. You may go to the greenhouse this morning."

I contentedly skipped the short distance to where my father worked, then fell to my knees next to him as he potted seedlings. The rich brown earth sifted through my fingers as I filled pots. Daddy planted each seedling, then poured over it a cup of water.

As we worked I asked, "Did you get to help your daddy when you were my age?"

"My father worked on the train as a fireman, so that was too dangerous for me to help. I brought him his lunch sometimes and got to see the big engines come puffing into the station, but then I had to go home."

"I'm glad that you don't work for the railroad!" I said as I handed him another filled pot.

"Well, I'm glad that your mummy still lets you come to the greenhouse after the scare you gave us the other day!"

On that memorable day, my sister Ruth had come with me to the greenhouse. We played ball inside while we waited for Daddy to call us to help. My sister threw a high ball to me. I ran backwards to catch it and toppled into the water trough. Ruth did not see me miss the ball, but at that moment, ran outside to see if Daddy was ready for us. When she returned to the greenhouse, at first she could not find me. Providentially, she caught sight of me submerged in the water tank.

"Daddy! Daddy! Come quickly!" Ruth shrieked.

He dashed in, pulled me out of the water, and pounded my back. After a few frightening moments, I coughed, sputtered, and gasped for breath.

Daddy wrapped me in a vegetable sack and prayed, "Help us, Lord. O, help us, Lord!" and quickly he rushed me home, where I was immediately put to bed. All through the night, my family kept a vigil to be sure I didn't develop pneumonia. Nor was I allowed to get up the next day. Gladys, my oldest sister, made a special trip home from work to care for me. She sat on my bed and braided my hair. Grace, my sister next in line, brought me tasty treats. Elsie read a story to me, and Ruth and I played Naught and Crosses (tic-tac-toe) most of the day.

The following day, my sister Grace brought me in a sweet pudding.

"Do you think when I get big I could be Daddy's helper?" I asked. "I don't want to go to somebody else's house and work like Gladys does."

"I don't know, Milly, dear, but get better today, and tomorrow Mummy will probably let you go back to the greenhouse."

Sure enough, the next morning, after Mother listened to my chest, she reluctantly gave me permission to return to the greenhouse. I flew like a bee to honey. "Hello, Daddy! I'm back!"

Father called from behind some tall tomato plants, "Milly, you may help prune. Eat all of the tomatoes that you can put your finger around. And after that, you may help me pull weeds around the green beans."

After I popped the last miniature tomato into my mouth, I joined Daddy outside. My mind was recalling a Bible story about Boaz and Ruth, which we had read at our family devotions the night before.

"Daddy, Boaz met Ruth in a field, didn't he? How did you meet Mummy?"

"When my family moved to England from Scotland, I attended the Baptist church that your mother's family, the Bennets and Castles, built. They owned the flour mill and a bakery. Being so important, they sat in the front pew of the church, and I, who was poor, sat in the back. During the services, I used to look at your mother's lovely brown hair, and think, "What a pretty girl!" Daddy's eyes got dreamy.

"And when church was over, I waited until her family passed my row, just in case her lovely blue eyes would notice me. My heart just bounced around inside of me whenever she did!"

"Did she wear pretty dresses?"

"I don't know, Milly. I met a farmer who told me about cows and their eyes."

"Cows and eyes, Daddy? We're talking about Mummy, not cows!"

"I know, dear, but the farmer taught me that the best cows, the ones that care for their calves, and give the best milk, all have kind, gentle eyes. The cows that should become roast beef, because they leave their calves and torment other cows, all have wild stares!"

"Daddy, do I have nice eyes?" I peeked over at him from the other side of the row of green beans.

"Just like your mother's."

I felt richer than a princess. "Did you marry Mother then, Daddy?"

"Not so fast as that, Milly! Your mother was engaged to another young man at church, whom her mother favored, so I was very sad. Then I didn't see her for a long time. She sailed to Canada to see her sister. While she was there, she decided she did not love her fiancee and canceled their engagement. Your mother wrote to me, and when she returned to England, we got married! We were poor, which did not please Mother Bennet, but we were happy." He was silent a moment, then said, "Our first unhappiness was when your big brother Cecil was born with Spina Bifida."

"What's that, Daddy?"

"That's where the spinal cord protrudes out of its place. Cecil wouldn't ever be able to walk or take care of himself. Your mother did everything for him until he died of measles when he was seven."

"Did Mummy cry?"

"Yes, she was grief stricken. After the funeral, your Mother sat alone in our bedroom for days until one morning your big sister Gladys came on tip-toe into the room and snuggled her way onto Mother's lap.

"'Why are you so sad, Mummy?' Gladys whispered.

"'Oh, my glad little girl. Mummy wanted Cecil to be strong and to grow and to serve God as Samuel did in the temple.'

"'But Mummy, I'm strong, and I'll serve God!' When Gladys said that, your mother was comforted."

I walked home that day thinking *I'll serve God, too. That makes Mummy happy.*

From an early age, I cried if my sisters got cross with each other. "Oh, Milly, stop bawling. You know we love each other! The Bible says, 'Be angry and sin not,' and we're not sinning," my sister Elsie said, exasperated with me.

"Leave her alone, Elsie. She was born in 1919 the Year of Peace so she's a Peace Baby and can't help it." Grace always stood up for me.

When I first started school, I cried and put up such a fuss in the classroom that I was taken outside to be with Grace. She had been called from her classroom to comfort me.

"Don't worry, Milly, dear, we'll soon be going home, and we'll pick flowers on the way! Be brave now and go and learn to read. You'll love reading, Milly."

With such comforting words, I was strengthened to return to my classroom.

Most of the literature that I learned to read came as Sunday school prizes. Every night, Daddy gathered us together in our "playroom." We sang, read stories to each other, prayed, and Father told us Bible stories. Grace had a lovely voice and often sang solos. In the winter months, when the days were short, we also played games: dominoes and ludo (after a dice is thrown, your man is advanced around a flat cardboard track). Also, we enjoyed Old Maid and Happy Families (memory games matching pictures on the cards). Other than these games, playing cards or alcoholic drink was not allowed in our home. Dolls also were forbidden, since they were considered to be too close to pagan idols. Years later, my father relented and let me have a doll. Grace gave it to me with a wardrobe, and I nearly worshipped it. . . .

Our parents regularly had little treats for us. Father kept pears, fresh year round, in a special box. He wrapped them in tissue paper and stored them in a cool place. Each evening, he brought out a few and cut us each a piece to eat. We were also given hard fruit candy that my parents ordered from the village grocer. Sometimes I provided the evening treat. Once in a while, I helped my father at the garden at the Big House. Mrs. Gordon-Brown's father, who lived with them, occasionally gave me a little box of Turkish delight. This exotic candy, which I passed around to my sisters until the rich sweets were gone, came in a round box.

The Big House

We were very proud of our father. One year he won first place in the Royal Chelsea Rose Show. He rode the train to London for the show and brought back a box of fancy chocolates. Each night we were allowed to choose a luscious brown sweet.

"Oh, they are all so scrumptious. Which one shall I take?" we asked as we debated the merits of one over another.

One night, Father went for the box and noticed empty spaces that were not there the previous evening. Father turned to us with an ashen face.

"Who has been into the chocolate box?" Utter silence met his question.

"Line up, please."

With the box in hand, he came before each of us. "Did you steal the chocolates?" Each of us claimed not to be guilty.

"'Thou God seest me,' children," he said seriously.

I pictured a big eye looking down from heaven. Since no one confessed, he examined our coats that hung on pegs in the hall. When he reached my older sister's coat, he discovered the wrappers to the chocolates. We all stood paralyzed. What would Father do? He went outside and cut a switch from a tree. Then in front of us, he switched my sister.

"'Thou shalt not steal'!" he commanded sternly as he applied the switch.

We all wailed our way to bed, overcome by grief and shame. It was as if he'd switched all four of us.

The next morning was Saturday, the busiest day of the week. As we routinely prepared for Sunday, no one mentioned the chocolates. Father polished everyone's shoes, and Mother baked. She made a roast for Saturday night with potatoes and vegetables that were always crisp, colorful, and delicious. After supper, she thinly sliced the leftover roast beef and made sandwiches for Sunday's lunch. Also in the basket for Sunday, she carefully arranged homemade sausage rolls, apple pies, and Dundee cake (a light fruitcake), which she had baked earlier in the day. We bathed, washed our hair, ironed, and mended the Sabbath day's clothing.

I mended clothing and could knit at the age of five. Marta, a German prisoner of war, who remained in England years after World War I, was my knitting teacher. My father trusted her and allowed her to become my friend. As we sat on our back doorstep, she taught me to knit.

"Marta, do you miss your family?" I asked her one day as I slowly twisted thick yarn around the long needle.

"*Ja, fraulein,* I do, but your vater has been very good to me, so I not complain," she said. "Most of my vamily they die. I know not vere to return. House burned up. One day maybe I go back and see." I sensed her sadness, set my needles down, reached up and gave her a childish cuddle.

As I grew older, I loved to climb our apple tree surrounded by a canopy of leaves. I would knit to my heart's content. To this day I knit the "German way" Marta taught me.

One day, from my lofty perch, I heard, "Mildred!"

Uh, oh. Mother used my full name. I must have done something wrong! I thought.

Quickly I climbed from the tree and ran to the front door.

"Yes, Mummy?"

"Put your needles and yarn down and get your dust cloth and follow me," she instructed.

She pointed to areas where that morning I had missed some dust. "A job worth doing is worth doing right, Milly. Cleanliness is next to godliness!" I quickly removed the errant dust.

One year later, when I was six, and mother was forty-eight, I would relinquish my title of "baby of the family." Mother was due to have another baby! In those days, when a woman was pregnant, a midwife came to stay at the home a few weeks before the due date, and stayed after for another few weeks. I did not care for the midwife who came to stay with us.

In the greenhouse, while I was working with my father, I asked, "Daddy, why is that lady staying in our house? She goes outside in the afternoon, and when she comes back, her breath smells funny, and she doesn't always walk straight. She isn't nice to us girls, Daddy."

"What do you mean, Milly?" Daddy stopped his work, waiting for my explanation.

"Well, she yanks really hard at our hair in the morning when it needs brushing, and she says that she is going to 'wop' it off. Does she mean she's going to cut it off, Daddy?"

"Don't worry, dear. Mummy needs her to help deliver the baby, so be patient for a few more days." I noticed that he didn't sing or hum for the rest of the day.

The next morning, as Ruth sat to get her hair brushed, our unwanted midwife drew a pair of scissors from her apron. One slash and a handful of long brown hair fell into Ruth's lap.

"What are you doing to my hair!"

"Doin' what should-a been dun 'ears ago, cuttin' the tangly stuff orf," she growled.

Ruth sat immobilized. At that moment, Elsie came into the room and stared, shocked at the short spears of hair that remained on Ruth's head.

"Sit ye dun," she ordered Elsie, and with one swoop from the scissors, Elsie's hair was gone.

"Do Mother and Father know what you're doing?" railed Elsie.

"I'm in charge 'ere now."

Grace and I entered the house at that moment, hand in hand. We were speechless as we viewed the floor covered with hair. The woman grabbed Grace.

"Oh, no you don't!" Grace screamed. She jerked back and ran for the front door. I was right behind her. The midwife caught my free hand, wrenched me loose from Grace's hold, slammed the front door shut, and pulled me back to the seat. Elsie and Ruth ran upstairs in torrents of tears. The midwife sheared me while I screamed vehemently. Just as the midwife was putting her shears away, the door swung open, and my mother waddled into the house. She had just come from the greenhouse, where she had been talking with Daddy.

"What *are* you doing, Miss Barnes?" Mother asked, aghast.

"Doin' ye a favor."

"But I . . . I . . . I didn't ask for any 'favors'!" Mother stumbled over the words.

"Wut's dun is dun," she retorted, and headed for the broom to sweep up the evidence.

That evening, there were many tears as each of us tried to work with what remained of our hair. During our family evening devotions, which Miss Barnes chose not to attend, she did not hear the lesson that Father taught us on forgiveness.

"'Pray for those who do you wrong,'" he advised us, "and that includes Miss Barnes. We still need her, children. The baby should be here any day, and then we can see her on her way."

A few days later, of all wonders, a boy was born! He was named John, and all of Miss Barnes' sins were forgotten with the thrill of his arrival.

The midwife stayed on for another week, until the day my father caught her in the field behind a tree with a bottle of whiskey. He invited her to leave immediately.

For a long time after John was born, Mother did not make the five-mile trek to church, but stayed home with the baby. One Sunday morning, we girls, in our Sabbath best, left the house fifteen minutes before our father. The walk, which included descending a steep hill, was through a gorgeous part of English countryside. However, we were cautious as we walked, since frequent rains left the ground soggy and muddy.

"Let's take a shortcut," I suggested, wanting to pick some bluebells I could see in the center of a field.

We carefully climbed over the fence and headed for the dancing flowers.

From some distance, I heard our father, "Get out of that field, quickly!"

I glanced back at him. He was waving his arms frantically and shouting, "Look behind you girls! Run, run!"

I turned around and saw a huge black bull rise from the grass. It put its head down and pawed the ground.

My legs felt like rubber as I dropped the blue flowers and raced after my sisters. We reached the fence and scrambled over it, the territorial beast just behind us. I gasped for breath as the snorting bull pawed the ground only a few feet away.

After we brushed each other off, though visibly shaken, we continued walking to church, where our father was a deacon. Both of our parents taught Sunday school. The minister of Burrough Green Baptist Church had baptized my parents and married them. A revered Bible teacher, he spoke so that even little girls could understand and remember his words. One of his sermons was taken from Nehemiah

8:10: "Eat the fat, and drink the sweet, and send portions unto them for whom nothing is prepared".

My father and mother took his lesson literally. Each Christmas, a blind woman and a poor family with five children, came to share our holiday "fat" and "sweet."

A few years after John's birth, Grace and Elsie left home to work for others, while Ruth and I became mother's helpers. One of the jobs that I had each day was to go for the milk from a farm a half mile away.

My sisters had bicycles that they earned, and I longed and prayed for one of my own. Our neighbor, Len Stead, who was the Brown's chauffeur, lived with his wife and little boy, Ron, in the other half of our landlord's worker's house. John often played with little Ron next door and learned unacceptable phrases and words. Every time we heard John come out with a dirty word, we told Mother. She did not believe us and said, "No, Johnny didn't say that! He couldn't!"

This denial frustrated me, and I wished that the Steads would move away, so that my brother would not continue to be badly influenced.

However, it was Mr. Stead who found a bicycle abandoned by the Brown children, brought it home, fixed it up, and gave it to me. I was ecstatic and quite amazed that God could use a foul-mouthed man who did not claim to be a Christian to answer my prayer!

It is not surprising that our beliefs affected our entire life. The public school that I attended was attached to the Church of England. The church dictated the hymns we sang and prayers said before class each morning. The ladies from that church also served the school children lunch.

"She's going to hell," I overheard one of my classmates tell her girlfriend out in the play yard. I turned and saw them point at me.

"I am not!" I gasped.

"Oh, yes you are! You weren't christened when you were a baby, were you?" They both started to taunt in unison, "Milly's going to hell. Milly's going to hell!"

"I am not! I don't know anything about being christened. I can't help what happened when I was a baby!"

Just then the teacher appeared and hurried us all inside. It didn't make a lot of sense to me that I should be penalized for something that I had been too young to control.

Since we were Baptists, my sisters had been allowed to drop out of the Church of England catechism class when they were in school. However, by the time I came along, the school officials decided, "Milly can just join in and learn the catechism!"

I was taught the sacraments and holy days, but when it came to participating in the rituals, such as Holy Communion, I was allowed to go home.

Domestic science was my favorite class at school. We were taken by bus to Burrough Green, which was an adventure in itself, where they had the facilities to teach us cooking. I often brought home little offerings.

"Daddy! Look what I made today!" I showed my father the cupcake with chocolate frosting and trims.

"Well, it looks nice, but who are you going to feed with that little piece? You can't feed a family with that much!" Everybody got a tiny spoonful and assured me that my culinary potential was great.

When I was ten, the minister at Burrough Green Baptist, Mr. Vine, went to India to do missionary work with his daughter. While he was gone, a Pentecostal tent meeting came to a neighboring village. My father and sisters went to the first service. Father did not go again, but he allowed my sisters to continue to go.

"Oh, Milly, dear! It was the most wonderful meeting I've ever attended! The singing had feeling in it, the praying was wonderful, and the preaching! Mr. Vine would have been moved by it!" Grace exclaimed. "I wouldn't miss a gathering under the tent for anything! And they believe in prophesying!"

"What's that?"

"That's when God uses someone to tell someone else something about themselves or about what's going to happen."

"Oh, like what? What did anyone prophesy?" I wanted details.

"Like Mr. Justin. He was told that he had constant headaches and that God wanted to heal him," Grace said.

"Well, does he have headaches? Did God heal him?"

"Yes! When Mr. Justin heard it, he started to cry. He said that he had not even told his wife about the headaches. Everyone gathered around him and put their hands on him and prayed."

"Did you touch him, Grace?"

"I sure did. And, Milly, he came back the next night with his whole family. The headache that had bothered him for weeks was completely gone, and he was so happy!"

"Did anyone else get a prophecy?"

"Yes, Miss Wilder was told to get right with God, as God could see the wrong things she was thinking and doing." Grace's face fell. "Afterwards, I prayed with her at the altar, and she said that she had been thinking about running away to London to live with a boy without being married."

Before we fell asleep that night, Ruth and I discussed what our older sisters had seen and heard. "I sure wish that I could go to one of those meetings," Ruth said.

"I'm not so sure," I admitted. "I try to be a good girl, but maybe somebody would say a prophecy over me about something I've done wrong. That would be scary. Daddy keeps talking about Jesus' coming again. I've been worried that if God should come, He might not even take me to Heaven!"

"Oh, Milly. Don't say that. You're scaring me. Go see if Daddy and Mummy are still here. Maybe they've already been taken and just you and I are left! Can you hear them? Are they talking?"

"Well, no, I can't hear them!"

"Oh, Milly, maybe they've been taken!" I went to the stairs and listened. Still no sound. I crept down the steps until I caught sight of Daddy's foot, then I raced back to Ruth and jumped under the covers. "They're still here!" Then we both snuggled under the covers and fell asleep.

A few days later, I was alone in the house, and there was a knock on the door. I opened it and recognized one of the ladies that Grace had told me about from the tent meetings. "I'm Miss Girdlestone," the refined, gray-haired lady said. "You must be Grace's sweet little sister, Milly. Have you ever given your heart to Jesus, dear?"

A little surprised, I replied honestly, "No, I haven't."

"Would you like to?"

She asked so gently, my response came spontaneously, "Yes, I sure would." I invited her into the playroom, and we both knelt.

"The Bible says in First John, chapter one," Miss Girdlestone began, "that if we confess our sins, He is faithful and just to forgive our sins. We humans are born in sin, shaped in iniquity, come into the world speaking lies, so it isn't that we have to think of every tiny sin we've ever done. We need to accept that Jesus paid for all of our sins, and our sinful nature. If your sister Grace brought you home a gift, you could not enjoy it until you took it from her outstretched hands. And how would she feel if you insisted on paying for her present or working for it? It is the same with God. He's offering salvation from sin as a free gift, and you need to accept it from Him and be grateful for His love."

"Milly, do you know John 3:16?"

"Yes, 'For God so loved the world . . .'" I started.

"I prefer to say it, 'For God so loved Milly, that He gave His only begotten Son, that if Milly should believe in Him, Milly should not perish, but Milly would have everlasting life. For God sent not His Son into the world to condemn Milly, but that Milly through Him might be saved!'"

It sounded so wonderful to me, that right there in the playroom, I prayed and told Jesus that I accepted the gift of forgiveness that He offered. "I am sorry for my sins, and thank you for dying on the cross to pay the price for them. I accept your gift."

I then turned to my new friend. "Thank you, Mrs. Girdlestone, I feel so much better!" After she left, I ran outside and danced around the yard, skipping and laughing with glee. I no longer had a heavy heart!

As the days passed, I desired to accompany Grace and my other sisters to the Pentecostal get-togethers. When I asked my father for permission, he hesitated.

"Well, Milly, there are things about those meetings that I'm not sure about, but if Grace is willing to take good care of you, and you really wish to go, you may."

"Oh, Daddy! Thank you, thank you, thank you!" I hugged his neck.

I could not get enough of the gatherings. I was sure that we were as the Christians in the time of the book of Acts. We sat in peace and silence at the weekly prayer meeting and prayed for those that came to mind. Sometimes a prophecy was said, sometimes a song was sung. Often there were tongues and interpretations. Each night we cycled back to our home, thrilled to have permission to attend.

Father met us at the door. "It's all right, speak in tongues all you like in that church, but here at home I want to see fruit!" We knew what he meant; he wanted to see the love, joy, peace, meekness, long-suffering, goodness, and gentleness (Galatians 5:22, 23) that to him meant more than outward religious excitements.

One prayer meeting night, since I was required to pick up the milk before preparing to go with my sisters, I grabbed the milk jug, jumped on my bicycle, and peddled for all that I was worth down the hill and around the first turn to the dairy farm. I put my head back and reveled in the breeze that blew through my hair. As I careened around another sharp turn, directly in front of me was another person on a bicycle. I rammed headlong into him. My bicycle, the milk jug, and I parted company in midair.

Collision

The man on the other bike was able to get up and come to the side of the path where I lay unconscious. He picked me up and carried me in the direction from which I had come. My sister Grace, just leaving for the prayer meeting, saw the stranger carrying me up the road. She called for my parents, and I was brought into the house and laid on the bed. Mother went for smelling salts while Grace hopped on her bike and raced to the prayer meeting. She burst into the quietness of the room and panted as she caught her breath, "Milly's been in an accident! She's unconscious!" Immediately, everyone took me to God in prayer.

Grace then got back on her bicycle and peddled home. She opened the door to our house and took two stair steps at a time to my bedroom. There she found me with a big smile on my face and a bowl of soup in my hand. "Hello, Grace. Sorry I missed the prayer meeting!"

"You were there, Milly, in every one's prayers!"

The following week, after prayer meeting, a few of us stopped to discuss the upcoming events. "We're going to put feet to our prayers. We've been wanting to evangelize our town, so next Saturday we're going to march through the streets as a group, carrying Christian banners!"

"What will be written on the banners?" the girl next to me asked.

"One will say: Prepare to meet thy God. Another: Sinners repent."

My sisters and I didn't have time to add to the conversation. We were expected at home. As we mounted our bicycles, Grace asked, "Don't you feel well, Milly? You look pale."

"Grace, how can I carry one of those signs down the street in front of my classmates? I'll die of fright and become one of our first martyrs." For the first time I thought about cycling really slowly to purchase the milk and missing the gathering altogether.

"'He who is ashamed of me is not worthy of me,'" Grace whispered the quote to me as I later said goodnight to her.

The week went by too quickly. I slowly joined the eager group at the church hall as they gathered and chose placards. A friend came over, dragging a sign too heavy for her. In bright red paint it read: Ye must be born again.

"Help me with this, Milly," she asked. I reluctantly took my half of the weight of the big sign as she proceeded to the front row of marchers. Someone started to sing. I decided that if I was going to be laughed at, there might as well be good reason. Courageously, I raised my head and sang with the others as we marched down the street. When it was all over, I realized that I had enjoyed myself and would be happy to do it again.

The more involved we got with this active Pentecostal group, the less Burough Green Baptist Church liked it. Father was unexpectedly invited to a deacon's meeting. "You do not have your house in order," the head deacon announced. "Your daughters are not in subjection, so unless you do something about it, we will accept your resignation."

Father said, "Well, my girls are saved, and that is all that matters." Mother and Father did not go to church for many years after that.

The leader of the tent campaign, a married man, to the horror of us all, got involved with a young girl of the group and left town with her.

Our father was beside himself. "That could have been one of you girls!"

When we were alone, I asked Grace, "What happened? How could something so ungodly occur in our midst?"

Grace replied, "How could Judas leave Jesus after walking with Him for three miraculous years, then kill himself? First Corinthians chapter five tells of a Corinthian Christian whose sin was so bad that Paul had to correct him in no uncertain words. How could that happen? I cannot explain it. All I can say is, if it happened to the early church, it can happen to us."

"What I have experienced these months has been real, and I can't turn away from it," Gladys said. As the little group faced community repercussions from the leader's immorality, the hurting little assembly grew closer and even more sincere.

That spring, we traveled by bus to London and met with other Pentecostals from all around the country in a big hall. As thousands of us raised our voices in songs of praise to God, it did not matter that we were called a cult or holy rollers. We were in God's presence, and our hearts thrilled and rejoiced at the pleasure of being so close to each other and to the One who had won our hearts, the Lord Jesus Christ.

A few months later, as we gathered in our little evening group, a prophecy came forth: "This little church will be closed, and you will be scattered to the ends of the earth."

This seemed unreasonable and impossible, but it happened sooner than we could have imagined. Gladys went to Bible School to become a missionary. Grace's employers moved to London and took her with them. Elsie and Ruth were offered better employment opportunities in London, so they submitted their resignations to Mrs. Gordon-Brown.

Since the Gordon-Brown estate was at that time having financial difficulties, they laid my father off and sold the property.

At this stressful time we received a letter from Grace.

Dear family,

I am keeping well and enjoying my new surroundings.

I was talking to a neighbor yesterday who has two young boys. She is quite desperate for help with them, and since Milly has turned fourteen, I thought of her. The lady seems kind, and I know Milly would get on well with the boys, as she does so well with our Johnny. I would be next door and could help her whenever and however she needed me.

Elsie is doing well. I heard her boss tell mine that she's never had such good home help in her life. You taught us well, Mummy!

Well, God bless you. Please take good care of each other for me.

Lovingly,
Grace

P. S. I have found a very satisfactory church.

As prophesied, before any of us could have worked it out, we were in the first stages of being scattered.

Goes to Work, 1933–1938

My little sister Joan danced around the backyard of our new home. Her golden curls flew as my brother Cliff and I watched from the kitchen window.

"Sis sure is glad Dad moved us to a home with a yard and grass and flowers, isn't she?"

"Yes, and Mum sure is thrilled with her new table and chairs!" I said as my hand touched the glossy wood of Dad's latest purchase.

"Don't touch the wood, Eddie. I just polished it!" Mum entered the room. "Supper will be ready in a twinkle, so why don't you boys go and wash up?"

Later, we sat down for our evening meal. My father asked me, "How are you doing in the new school, Eddie?" Mother scooped a generous portion of greens onto my plate.

About as good as these greens, I thought, but replied, "Okay, I guess."

"How about you, Cliff?"

"Oh, it's great. My class is just getting introduced to algebra, which I like a lot. I've got a question on my homework, though." He turned to me, "Eddie, could you help me with it?"

"Not if it's in algebra. I could help you in art or woodwork, but algebra might as well be Greek, for all I'm understanding it. Back in Bow I never knew algebra existed."

Mother watched me push the food around on my plate and thought a change of subject was in order, "Eddie, what about the new church? I've been too busy getting settled to go. Do you like it?"

"Yes, it's fine, though the Sunday school teacher is a little fanatical. He's constantly saying that we've got to get 'saved.' Saved from what? If he said it was being saved from algebra, I'd take him up on it!"

After supper, I followed my father into a corner of the living room, where he had a bench set up for fixing typewriters. He sat down and picked up a wrench. "You're always busy, aren't you, Dad?"

"That's how we were able to move, and that's how I'm able to get nice things for your mother and you children." He did not look up but applied the wrench to the machine in front of him.

"Dad, I don't like school. I'll soon be fourteen, and you and I could start a typewriter business together. I've watched you for years, and I've learned a lot. We would do really well together!"

"I don't know, Eddie," he murmured, intent on the repair.

"'I am the master of my fate, I am the captain of my soul!' That's what William Henley said in the Invictus. We don't have to work for a boss. We could do great things together!"

"What will be, will be, Eddie."

Frustrated, I left the room muttering, "Yes, it jolly well will be, unless you're willing to change it!"

In June I turned fourteen, and by the end of summer, Father moved us again, this time to a better home and neighborhood in Coulsdon, surrounded by hills and woods. The fresh air, the gentle rustle of the trees, the colors of the abundant flowers, the uncluttered surroundings, filled me with the joy of being alive.

To complete my contentment, Father asked me shortly after we had settled in, "How would you like to work at a typewriter factory, Eddie?"

"I would like that very much!"

"A man from the Oliver Typewriter Company sat beside me on the bus today. He said that his company is hiring machine workers. I told him how good you are with your hands, so he's going to see about getting you on."

Two weeks later, I took a bus to my first job. The room that I reported to was full of loud machines. Belts and pulleys stretched from floor to ceiling. The machinery intrigued me, but the boss, a burly, foul-mouthed man, created a miserable atmosphere.

After a week of training, he said, "Ware, I want you to take this box of levers over to machine two and thread the holes into them."

An hour later I returned with the job done. "Here they are, sir."

He cursed. "You couldn't possibly have those finished in such a short time." He grabbed the box and proceeded to examine each piece. Again he swore. "Here's another box. Do the same to them."

The unpleasant harangue continued from day to day. The only feedback I received was the boss's amazement at what I could do and subsequent bigger requirements of me.

On Sundays, I took respite from the week's frustrations and attended the Coulsdon Baptist church.

"You certainly seem to spend a lot of time with the Sunday afternoon Bible class," Mother mentioned one day as I came into the house from a rugby game.

"They are an educated, high-society group, Mum, and they've accepted me. They call me Edward. I sure like that better than Eddie."

The next Sunday afternoon, our young men's group had a guest speaker, Mr. Arthur Halliday. He was short, well groomed, and delivered an in-depth Bible study on the imminent return of the Lord. At the conclusion of his discourse, he asked the entire class, "Would you young men like to come to my home today for tea?" This was completely unexpected. We glanced at each other. Since we had nothing planned, we accepted his invitation.

"I hope his wife will be a good sport when we all land at her doorstep," Roger, one of the young men, commented as we walked along behind the country gentleman.

"I hope she's a good cook," I countered as we turned into Mr. Halliday's front gate.

As the gate clicked behind us, I saw movement at the window, and the front door opened. A sweet little lady was introduced as "Mrs. Halliday." She received us graciously and invited us into their living room where a little boy about the age of my sister Joan was standing. "This is our son, John."

Suddenly, the kitchen door opened and four girls, like stair steps, entered the room. Mr. Halliday explained, "I have five daughters. This is Gladys, Grace, Elsie, and Ruth."

They nodded and smiled.

Once again the kitchen door opened and the fifth girl appeared. I caught a glimpse of the blue of heaven in her eyes. *What a lovely girl*, I thought. "Gentlemen, this is Milly," Mr. Halliday proudly announced. I couldn't take my eyes off her as she set a tray on the table. She glanced up shyly, and her gentle eyes met mine. I was no longer interested in the sandwiches, the flavor of the cake, or what we were drinking. When the meal ended, I remained in the room, while my pals filed out, heartily thanking our host and hostesses.

My mind raced as I considered how I could stay long enough to speak with my beautiful young hostess. Just then, she began to clear the table and passed right by me.

"Excuse me, would you come to church with me?" I blurted. This sudden invitation must have surprised her. Her cheeks turned a pretty pink.

"Why, yes, I could do that, " she murmured shyly, and continued to clear the table.

"Thank you! Thank you!" I beamed as I made my way out the door.

Work went faster for me that week as I anticipated Sunday.

On the appointed day, I nervously knocked on the Halliday door. My heart skipped extra beats as she joined me for the walk to church. On the way home, she agreed to accompany me the following week, and then again the next week.

As I walked her home the third time, she surprised me by asking, "Eddie, would you do something for me?"

"Why, yes, of course. What is it?" I would have been happy to trek deserts without water or scale the highest mountains without shoes.

"Would you come to my church?"

"Your church? What church is that?"

"A Pentecostal church," she replied.

My mind raced. I thought she was Baptist like her father. I had heard Pentecostals were a cult, rolled on church floors, and had no church manners at all. As we neared her house, I decided quickly, "Okay, I'll come with you this once."

She looked happy, and we discussed the details of when and where we would meet.

All through that week I worried about the Pentecostals and their church habits. The next Sunday, I met her in the front of their simple church building as we had agreed. We entered the vestibule, and several people came up to us and shook my hand. "God bless you! Thank you for coming."

We found a seat and the meeting began with some exuberant choruses, after which people gave testimonies of what God had done for them. I listened in awe. Before I knew it, the minister was up front introducing his topic, Hell. He began to elaborate on this place: its heat, its horror. He paced from one side of the altar to the other. "Hell is real. Hell is hot! And there's only one way to keep away from there."

I trembled in my shoes and thought, *"Well, for God's sake, hurry up and tell me!"*

"Jesus is the only escape. You must accept that Jesus died on the cross to rescue you. He paid the complete price on Calvary. Raise your hand if you want to accept his free gift of salvation!"

My arm shot up. I wished to be saved. Somehow this minister was able to get through to me what my Sunday school teacher had tried to do for many months.

Milly and I skipped along the pavement as if angels carried us toward home that night. I saw her to her front door.

"Eddie, you have made me so happy that I could burst," she beamed and then disappeared behind the door.

I rushed home, anxious to share the good news with my family. I found my parents comfortably situated in front of the living room fire. "Dad! Mum! I'm saved!"

"Oh, that's nice, Eddie. There's some cake on the table if you wish," Mother said.

"Cake . . . Mother, you must not have heard me! I'm saved from hell!"

But she *had* heard me. I felt frustrated and alienated. My parents did not understand what I was telling them; just as I had not understood what my Sunday school teacher had been teaching for several months. Why could they not respond to my excitement, even if they did not understand?

Milly and I visited each other's churches regularly. Once, I invited her to a missionary service at my church. The guest speaker was an enthusiastic German woman, Miss Alma Doering. She waved her middle-aged hand at us. "I have trekked across Africa three times," she said, as I visualized her thin legs wading through marshes, "and the need is very great. So great that I have cried and cried to the Lord for more workers. Young people with more physical strength than I. The Bible says, 'Say not ye there are yet four months, then cometh harvest' (John 4:35). The harvest is ready now. People are dying without Christ as I speak!"

Miss Alma Doering's stirring words went to both our hearts. At the invitation, we walked forward, hand in hand, to dedicate our lives to be missionaries. Following our dedication, Milly and I discussed our leaving to go to Africa as early as possible.

A retired missionary heard of our zeal and spoke to me. "Eddie, I advise that you go to Bible School in order to prepare yourself for the work."

I listened to his advice and wrote to the school he suggested. I gave them all of the information that they might need for my admission. After posting the letter, I ran from the bus stop up the hill to our home every day to see whether I had received a response.

A few months later, a letter arrived. I grabbed the missive from the mantel, where my mother had put it, and ran out the back door. Flossy, now slow and gray, licked my hand as I plopped down on the grass beside her and opened the letter. My hands trembled as I read:

Dear Mr. Ware,

We appreciated your letter and are delighted with your enthusiasm, but the truth is, you are too young to start Bible school. Possibly in four years, when you are eighteen, you could apply again.

My mind reeled. "I thought that souls were dying, Flossy! What does that have to do with how old I am?"

Later that evening, I showed the letter to Milly. She, too, was discouraged.

"I guess all we can do is be missionaries here," she sighed.

We started to look for opportunities to witness for Christ in our own backyards. I learned that the young men's Sunday school class was going on the street to witness as a group, so I decided to join them. We stood on a corner in town and sang and read portions from the Bible. Milly's oldest sister, Gladys, saw us and asked if she could join us. We were glad for the company. After a few minutes, she asked timidly, "May I say a little something?"

"Well, yes. Certainly you may."

Before our eyes, a diminutive woman was transformed. Her eyes shone as she spoke with fervor, "Now, none but Christ can satisfy, no other name for me! I've found life and peace and lasting joy in Jesus."

I watched in amazement. I recalled that Gladys also wanted to be a missionary. Her plans to go to China were prevented by circumstances.

Nevertheless, she continued to work tirelessly for others. To her family's dismay, she often brought unwed mothers home with her. Since she generously gave her money and possessions to others in need, she owned nothing. Even though her family sometimes thought that her unselfish generosity was extreme and fanatical, her sincerity was admired.

My joy during these weekends of service and work with the church youth group did not carry over during the week. I found it difficult to think positively about my job. Furthermore, I was frustrated by the difficult challenge to win my heathen employer to Christ.

He was totally unreasonable. Daily, he gave me enormous boxes of small machine parts to assemble, and then cursed me for completing the assigned task!

Finally, after tolerating too much abuse, I shared with my dad that I was unhappy with my employer and my job and explained the reasons. Within a short time, he found employment for me at another office machine factory where I learned to hand make templates.

Anxious for me to advance in my career, some months later, Father asked me to consider a new opportunity. "How would you like to go each morning on the Workman's train to downtown London and learn to operate and repair calculators?"

"Calculators are new and exciting. I would love the job!"

I was employed there for only one year, when I was offered employment at the same company where my father worked. Eagerly, I accepted this new opportunity and became proficient in repairing and assembling typewriters.

During these busy years of advancement, I saw less and less of Milly. One day, as I walked to the train on my way home from work, I saw an old acquaintance from Bow, the little girl that I had stolen flowers for. "Well, hello Eddie! How are you?" she said, her eyes searching mine for the old spark.

"Oh, hello Jean. You're looking good." She had grown into an attractive young woman with the wavy brown hair, dancing eyes, and trim figure that I remembered.

"I sure missed you after you left Bow."

I didn't want to tell her that I hadn't thought of her. "That's nice! What are you doing these days?"

"I'm a seamstress at Cohen's."

The memory of the place gave my stomach a pleasant flip. "I used to live right across from there!"

"Yes, I know. I think of you when I pass your old house."

We were standing in front of a movie theater. "Uh, how would you like to go to a picture show with me?"

Soon we were seeing a lot of each other, while thoughts of Milly drifted farther and farther from my mind. I didn't go to church as often, and Jean never went.

Money soon became more important to me. I realized that a mechanic's wages provided a steady job, but not the extras I wanted. Therefore, I applied for the position of a typewriter salesman within the company. I also took side jobs and quickly increased the amount of money that went through my pocket.

One payday, I bought a motorcycle that didn't run and spent hours working on the engine in our front yard. I was excited about my progress, but found my father did not share my enthusiasm. "Eddie, you must get that eyesore out of our yard. I have not worked all these years to live in a garage now!"

Mother overheard his comment and mentioned softly as he entered the house, "What about the typewriters you brought home when we lived in Bow, Joe?"

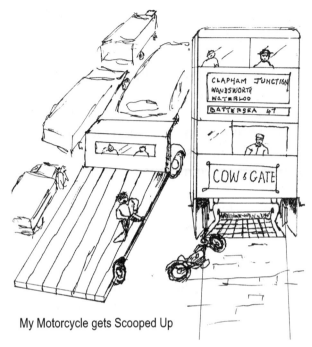

My Motorcycle gets Scooped Up

Father did not mention the motorcycle again for a week, so I was able to get the two-wheeled wonder working. I decided to ride it to London to work.

"The train is much more dependable, Eddie. You had better not let that contraption make you late to work!"

"I'll be early!" I said, and gave Mother a hug as I ran out the door.

It took longer to start than I expected, and I left the yard just as my father headed for the train. The wind tossed my hair, and the roar of the engine put me into a world all my own; I was a free man.

The traffic increased the closer I got to downtown. Cars honked at me. A taxi cut me off. I focused on survival, as fast cars and impatient drivers made driving a nightmare.

Suddenly I saw a tram heading towards me. I looked down, and to my horror, saw that I was riding on the tram tracks! At that moment, I saw my escape. An empty flatbed truck rumbled along the lane next to me. In a split second, I saved my life. I leaped off the motorbike onto the flat bed of the truck. At that same instant, the tram dropped its cow catcher, flipping my motorcycle into the air. Traffic screeched to a halt. Alive and unhurt, I took the break in the traffic flow to jump off the truck and mount my motorcycle that was lying on the street beside the tram tracks.

"Watch where you're going young man! Next time you'll get killed!"

Similar warnings bounced off me as I kicked the starter. The engine revved, and I pulled over into the traffic lane, pleased with my agility.

My father was not impressed when I walked in late for work. He was aware of all that I did and did not do. I resented the surveillance and made up my mind to get away from it.

One day, as I listened to the world's problems being discussed by fellow workers, I found the solution.

"War is inevitable," one said.

"Yes, I agree," said another. "Hitler is begging for a fight. He's pretty cocky to take us on. Wasn't the Great War enough to teach the Germans that we're hard to beat?"

"What worries me," the first fellow continued, "is what will happen to our business when we all get conscripted. Of course, all of the young men will go first, but how much time will we be given?"

I decided that it was better to join the forces now and have a choice than to wait and be made a foot soldier. My father had been a German prisoner of war in the "war to end all wars," and I did not wish the same experience.

My first love was the navy. At lunch hour, I went to the recruiting office and was told, "I'm sorry, young man, but your eyesight is not good enough. We can't take you in the navy."

Crestfallen, I thought, "Well, if the navy doesn't want me, I'll try the air force." The air force was impressed with my mechanical background, and signed me up on the spot. I was eighteen.

Leaves Home to Work, 1933–1942

"But Mr. Darby, I'm so worried. What is Mrs. Mason like? And will she like me?"

The new Austin putted along the narrow lane to the great city of London, where I was to enter my first job away from home.

"Milly, dear, you are such a pet, no one could help but love you. Mrs. Mason is a cultured English lady who has had a tragic thing happen to her."

Mr. Darby, the head of the home where Grace worked, slowed the car around a sharp curve. He and his wife had offered me a ride to their neighbor, who was my new employer, in London.

"A few years ago, her husband abandoned her for a young secretary. Since then, she has been consumed with shame and hatred." He paused, then continued, "She has removed every memory of him from her home and life; pictures of him have all been destroyed. Her problem is that Graham, their youngest son, looks, and often acts, just like him. However, Jeffrey, the oldest, has her features and mannerisms."

I twisted my handkerchief into knots as I wondered how I would fit into Mrs. Mason's circumstances.

Mr. Darby changed the subject. "I have heard of a position in London that sounds perfect for your father's talents. Coulsdon Purley Council is looking for a gardener."

"Oh, how wonderful! Then I would be able to see them on my days off!"

Before I knew it, Mr. Darby parked the car in front of a big home that stood apart from the rows of houses that lined other London streets.

"Well, here we are! This is the Mason house!" Everything seemed formidable, except the flowers that smiled a welcome to me from the front yard. Mr. Darby ushered me up the front steps.

An elegant lady met us at the door. She stretched out her fair hand and shook my damp palm. "I'm Mrs. Mason, and I'm delighted to meet you. I know we shall get along well. I have heard many nice things about you."

From behind her skirt, I saw the mischievous eyes of a little boy with a tussled mop of brown hair. "Graham, quit hiding!" Mrs. Mason said sternly. The little head disappeared.

"Never mind. Now that you are here, Milly, things should improve. I understand that you have a remarkable way with little boys. Please come in, and we'll take your bag right upstairs to your bedroom."

Mr. Darby excused himself and left for an appointment. With a lump in my throat, I waved as the Austin disappeared around the corner. Mrs. Mason led me up the stairs. "I hear you come from a big family. You will miss them, of course, but I hope that you will enjoy being with the boys and me." Her kind words gave me courage.

My bedroom was lovely, with lace curtains and fine furniture. As I walked around in awe, Mrs. Mason pointed through the open window to a large home up the street. "That is the Darby's residence where your sister Grace works. I believe that the top window facing yours is her room."

Just then a loud *thump* sounded from downstairs. Mrs. Mason looked heavenward and her mouth tightened. "He's incorrigible," she said. She turned and walked to the doorway. "Graham! You know those toys are not to come upstairs. Take them outside immediately!" The noise receded with the little boy's footsteps.

"Your main job, Milly, will be to keep track of Graham. You will find him difficult at best. Jeffrey is older and much easier. I understand that you are very good with your brother, and that is how I want you to be with my boys. "

"Thank you, I will enjoy that," I assured her, since I had already fallen in love with the little truant during the few glimpses I'd had of him.

"Let's go down and discuss my other expectations over a cup of tea. You can settle in later this afternoon."

We drank a cup of tea in the sunny kitchen and talked about food and how she wanted it prepared; the house, and what duties I was to perform in its upkeep. It occurred to me that Mrs. Mason did not intend me to be a servant, but a helper, and if I fit in, a part of the family.

"I bathe in the morning, and you may bathe in the afternoon. I expect you to take a two-hour rest every afternoon."

"Oh, but I don't need a rest. I keep busy all day!"

"Well, here you will have two hours during the day to yourself. I advise that you use them to rest. When the boys get in from school, you will need your wits about you. Jeffrey gets in at five and Graham at three-thirty."

She glanced into the backyard and frowned as Graham stacked his toys, then like a mountaineer, stood on top of the heap and waved his hands.

"Did you say I could treat the boys as my own brothers?"

"Please, they will enjoy it!"

I collected our empty teacups and took them to the sink. Mrs. Mason returned the biscuit tray to its shelf.

"If I need you, Milly, I will ring this little bell." She showed me a dainty china bell that had a pleasant chime to it. "I despise shouting and loud noises."

Suddenly, we heard a terrific din. We looked outside. Graham was throwing his stack of toys at a metal bucket. To save his mother's nerves, I slipped out the back door and called his name.

"Hello, Graham. Come and meet me!"

He shuffled over. "Mummy says I'm a no-good ruffian," he announced, "so I am!"

"Well, let me look at you. I know quite a lot about little boys. Hmmm, let's see now." I turned him slowly around and examined him. "Yes, hmmmmm. I would say, yes indeed, I would say that you are . . . smart. Am I right?" I asked as I continued with my inspection. "And clever, and fun, and the nicest little boy in this whole neighborhood!" By this time his mouth was open and his eyes were wide.

"I like you," he whispered. Graham and I were inseparable from then on. I woke him each day, made his breakfast, walked him to school, and met him again in the afternoon. We played games and took long walks. I helped him with his homework, made sure he bathed, and that he kissed his mother before bedtime. Each night, I read him a story or two, sang a song, prayed a prayer, and gave him a big hug before I turned out his bedroom light.

Mrs. Mason gave me every Wednesday and Sunday afternoon off to spend with my sisters. Mr. Darby, true to his word, had found my father the job in Coulsdon, so my sisters and I regularly went to visit our parents. Our father was happy with his work and with his welcome at the Coulsdon Baptist church, where he was often asked to teach the Sunday school classes.

One Sunday afternoon, Gladys, Grace, Elsie, Ruth, and I all arrived at our parents' home for afternoon tea. Gladys was in her second year of Bible school and often brought other Bible school students home to tea. This time she arrived alone, which the rest of us preferred.

"Oh, Mummy, it is so nice to see you!" I hugged my dear mother. "Where's Daddy?"

"He was invited to speak to the afternoon Young Men's class at church. It should be over soon, and he'll be home. He's enjoying ministering again."

"Does he still pray and read his Bible in the rose garden, like he did back at the Gordon-Brown estate?"

Before I got my answer, I glanced out of the window and saw my father coming down the sidewalk with at least eight young men following behind. "Mother! What is this?"

"What, dear?" mother came to the window and watched as father turned into the yard. "Daddy must have invited his class home. That's unusual. Hurry, Milly! I'll answer the door, and you and your sisters do something in the kitchen!"

I dashed for the kitchen, where my sisters had started to put our meal together. "Daddy's brought company home! Get another pot of tea going, and bring out Mummy's cake tin."

"Who are they," asked Grace, "the minister and his wife?"

"It looks like the group of young men Daddy's teaching." I brought more bread for Elsie to slice.

Ruth peeked into the entryway through the crack in the kitchen door. "There are nine young men!"

John, our little brother, swung the door wide open as he entered the kitchen. "Looks like Father's brought you each home a husba . . ." Grace cupped her hand over his mouth. I quickly swung the door closed. Elsie nearly fainted, and Gladys tried hard not to laugh hysterically.

Mother appeared at the kitchen door. "John, pick some berries from the garden. Girls, as soon as the food is ready, bring a tray into the dining room. Daddy wants to introduce you."

"Would it be asking too much, Mummy, if we prepared the food, and you served it?" Elsie asked.

"No. Father asked that each of you come out." She returned to her job as hostess.

"All right, you go first, Gladys." Grace gave the sandwich tray to her older sister and grabbed the teapot. Elsie took up the sugar bowl and creamer and was at Grace's heels. Ruth had the cake platter and was out the door behind Elsie. I saw I had nothing to carry. Then the back door banged shut. John entered with a basket of berries. His mouth was pink. "Are they good, Johnny?" All he could do was nod, as he was chewing a juicy berry. I took the basin of fruit from him, rinsed the berries and arranged them on a plate.

When I entered the dining room, I noticed that the young men were on their feet and the last one had just given Ruth a handshake. I turned a few shades of pink when Daddy announced, "This is my youngest daughter, Milly."

I managed to shake each hand timidly and sat down where Mother directed. I glanced across the table and caught a twinkle in the eyes of a curly-headed boy, Edward Ware.

Daddy's guests stayed for an hour. As they were leaving, Grace and I cleared the table. I turned with an arm full of plates and found myself face to face with young Mr. Ware.

"Excuse me, but would you come to church with me next week?" he asked.

I nearly dropped the plates back onto the table and felt my cheeks warm up. "Why . . . yes, I could do that."

After he left, I berated myself. *Why did I say that I would go? I don't even know him! He might not even be a Christian.* (I had been taught strictly to never go out with a boy unless he was a Christian.) *But why would Daddy bring him home if he weren't? He attends the Bible class!*

The next Sunday, I wore my best dress and fidgeted with my hands as Grace and I traveled back to our parents' home. "Milly, you seem nervous. Did you have a hard week at Mrs. Mason's?"

"No," I answered. "One of Daddy's Sunday afternoon Bible class boys asked me to go to church with him this week, and I said that I would."

A few months earlier, a young man, Percy, at the Pentecostal church was interested in me. When Grace found out, she had reacted like a mother hen and worried me constantly with advice.

As I expected, Grace asked, "Is he born again, Milly? Make sure that he doesn't get too close to you!" She continued to preach to me until he arrived. I whisked him out the door immediately.

"It's a pretty day, isn't it?" I remarked as the front door closed behind us.

"Yes, it is." He took up the conversation and began asking about my work and telling me about his job. On the way home from church, we continued to learn about one another. He said that I could call him Eddie as his parents did, instead of Edward as the boys did. I liked his gentlemanly manner and his knowledgeable, bright outlook on things. As we approached my parents' gate, he asked if he could accompany me again the next week. "Yes," I conceded. He smiled and his eyes shone.

We attended the Baptist church together for three weeks. I enjoyed both his conversations and attention. In our conversations, I noticed that he never brought up Bible topics. This concerned me, since each week Grace quizzed me about whether he was truly a Christian. And also Mrs. Mason warned me, "You don't want to be going out with that young man too often."

The following week, I asked Eddie if he would attend my church for a change. He seemed a little reluctant but agreed.

That Sunday, as we entered my church, many people smiled at Eddie and shook his hand. When the service commenced, Eddie joined in the hymns, but did not seem to know many of the choruses. As the minister prepared to speak, we gave him our undivided attention. He spoke on hell. Eddie started to perspire. At the end of the sermon, the speaker invited anyone who wished to become a Christian to raise his hand. Eddie raised his arm up immediately. All the way home, his face was radiant, and he was so excited that he could hardly sit still on the bus seat. "Oh, Milly! I'm saved! Really and truly saved from that horrible place of hell!"

From then on, Grace became fond of Eddie and always made him welcome. On my days off, we spent many hours together, walking or biking for miles over the beautiful English Downs. "Do you mind if I hold your hand?" Eddie asked me one delightful day.

"It would be all right," I answered. We shared our dreams and hopes and plans for the future as we walked.

One Wednesday, he invited me to attend his church, since there was to be a guest missionary speaker. We sat together in one of the front row seats and listened intently to a white-haired lady make Africa and its natives come to life.

"These fields of human souls are white already to harvest," she told us. John 4:35 was her text. Edward's hand clutched mine as the earnestness of her appeal stirred our hearts. She asked if anyone wanted to dedicate their lives as laborers in God's great mission field. We responded and walked hand in hand down the aisle to answer the appeal and to have her pray for us. When we left the church that night, we knew we would never forget the speaker, Miss Alma Doering.

Eddie started to read every book he could get his hands on about missionaries and foreign countries, particularly the continent of Africa. He read of leprosy colonies where people's hands, noses, and feet fell off; of cannibals who had an appetite for white missionary stew; of snakes and lions that tried to share space in missionaries' grass-roofed shacks; of alligators and rhinoceroses that tipped missionary boats over. As we discussed these future difficulties, it appeared to me that Eddie's biggest concern was whether I would be able to handle my part. "Now, Milly, are you sure that you won't mind washing clothes in a river?"

"I will have a native worker come with me and shout if she sees alligators, just in case I'm too busy washing," I assured him.

"And what about sewing? Can you make me shirts?" He was worried that his clothing would wear out and mosquitoes and leeches would then feast on his exposed flesh.

"Eddie, I have been sewing since I was little, and I will bring a whole packet of needles and several spools of thread when we go."

We met a retired missionary from Africa, Dr. Morton, and spent many Sunday afternoons in his home, listening breathlessly to his missionary experiences. On one occasion, an inch-and-one-half-long June bug crawled past Dr. Morton's chair as he told one of his stories. Without a hesitation in his voice, he picked the insect up between his thumb and forefinger, and squeezed it until it popped, then he flicked it into the fire.

Our young English sensibilities were shaken to their depths. As we walked home, awed by what we had witnessed, I asked, "Eddie! Do you think that you'll be able to do that to bugs?"

"I'm not sure, but at least he didn't eat it!"

As the months passed, it became obvious that we could not leave for the foreign mission field immediately. Not only were we not prepared to deal with bugs, but no opportunity opened to us. We were told that we were too young, too poor, and too needed where we were. Also, Eddie's job was more demanding. At that time, Mrs. Mason required more of my time, so Eddie and I saw less and less of each other.

I thoroughly enjoyed life at the Masons, although my heart ached for Graham. It hurt as I saw him and his mother grow farther apart.

The final cruel blow came when Mrs. Mason called me into her bedroom and announced, "I am going to send Graham to a boarding school." Her bitterness would now inflict more hurt and pain upon an innocent boy.

"But, Mrs. Mason, why?"

"He needs a better education."

"Is Jeffrey going too?" I inquired.

"No, of course not. Jeffrey is in track and enjoys where he is, so I wouldn't consider it." I bit my lip to hold back the tears.

Mrs. Mason made the arrangements for his departure. "I shall miss you, Milly," Graham told me as he sat on the edge of my bed the day before he was to leave.

"And I, you." Tears ran down my cheeks.

"I shall write to you every week," he promised, "and tell you all about what I'm doing."

True to his word, he wrote to me every week. Since he never corresponded with his mother, she read my letters to learn how he was adjusting and performing in his school-work.

After Graham left, I took over other jobs for Mrs. Mason. I went to the bank, ran errands, cooked meals, helped to entertain, and cleaned house. My employer was always kind and appreciative of my efforts. In the afternoons, she played the piano and lulled me to sleep with the classics. In the evenings, she helped me learn my alto part for the Elim Church choir. My sisters and I all sang in the church choir. In January, the Elim choirs across the country were assigned to practice a regimen of songs, which were chosen by the main choir in London. Triumphant hymns, such as *Up From the Grave He Arose,* and *Guide Me, O Thou Great Jehovah.*

These hymns were sung across the country in small groups until the Monday after Easter, a national holiday. On that date, all of the congregations converged in London's Royal Albert Hall, composing a choir of thousands. Ronald Cooper, a gifted organist, played the huge pipe organ, which vibrated like thunder with angelic majesty. The mass choir, dressed in white, with wide, blue ribbons across our chests, sang each of the three services. A baptismal service followed the final service.

"Grace, I want to be baptized," I announced resolutely on the second day of the meetings.

"Wonderful, Milly! The Bible says very clearly that we should be baptized. Acts 2:38, 'Repent and be baptized every one of you in the name of Jesus Christ for the remission of sins, and ye shall receive the gift of the Holy Ghost.'

Also, Matthew 28:19, where Jesus told His disciples to 'teach all nations, baptizing them in the name of the Father, Son, and Holy Ghost.'"

I was one of hundreds baptized by George Jeffries. I wondered how he had the strength to baptize so many. He stood in the tank, specially brought in for the baptisms, and individually dipped each person completely under the water. When it came my turn, I was joyful for this opportunity to follow God's Word in obedience.

I returned to Mrs. Mason's, exuberant from these church experiences. "It was wonderful!" I said. "There were people healed and helped. One man was an alcoholic at last year's meeting. He had lived on the streets of London, but since last year's meeting, he has not touched alcohol. As a matter of fact, he said that the desire completely left him, and he's holding down a job at the fruit market! Another woman was paralyzed all her life, but after prayer . . ."

"Milly, those are just fairy tales!" Mrs. Mason interrupted me. "You're too young to understand what is really going on."

"But, Mrs. Mason, this is real. I saw and heard it myself!" She picked up a magazine. The conversation was closed.

Often I had heard Mrs. Mason mumble, "He's going to pay."

"Who's going to pay, Mrs. Mason?" I asked innocently one day.

"That husband of mine. If it takes until I'm ninety, I will make him sorry." Even though she did not need any of his money, she was determined to inflict vengeance by compelling him to compensate her. "I despise him and what he's done to our family."

After Graham was sent to boarding school, Jeffrey began to stretch his masculine wings and to ask questions that both Mrs. Mason and I found uncomfortable. "The boys were teasing me today because I don't know enough differences between girls and boys. I don't know how babies are made!" Jeffrey wailed to his mother.

"Don't worry, Jeffrey. We'll find someone to help us with this," she assured him.

Mrs. Mason began an intense search for an appropriate male figure to advise the fatherless boy. A few days later, she rushed into the house proclaiming, "I've found him! He's perfect, and he's willing!"

"Who's perfect?"

"The new vicar of Sanderstead. He has a real way with youth. Apparently, he lost his two sons to meningitis, and since then, takes all needy boys as his own. I had an interview with him and asked him, 'How could you still believe in God when He let your boys die?' He told me a queer thing, 'God is God. He is Absolute and I will not question Him.'" She stopped at this point and looked out of the window for a few seconds. "I spoke with him about Jeffrey, and he promised to help us. Jeffrey has an appointment with him tomorrow." Mrs. Mason looked relieved and happy.

The next night, Jeffrey returned from his interview and raved over his newfound friend. "He's wonderful, Milly! He answered all of my questions and helped me understand so many things about my father and mother. He said I needed to become a Christian; that Jesus was knocking on my heart's door, and that He wanted to come in and help me. I had to answer the knock and invite him in, as he would not force Himself into my heart. So I invited Him in!"

"Wonderful, Jeffrey!" I jumped up and hugged him.

"Reverend Rose said he had a special verse just for me," Jeffrey said.

"Which one?"

"Joshua 1:8, 'This book of the law shall not depart out of thy mouth; but thou shalt meditate therein day and night, that thou mayest observe to do according to all that is written therein: for then thou shalt make thy way prosperous, and then thou shalt have good success.' And, Milly," Jeff went on, "you should have heard Mr. Rose tell how he became a Christian."

"How was that?"

"Well, he was a captain in the war, in charge of a platoon of soldiers, and was commanded to take his men farther into France. They marched down a road that came to a fork. The left road was loud with artillery fire and obvious action. The right was peaceful and looked like the better way. As he stopped to decide which way he should lead his men, he heard a distinct voice tell him to go left. As his men reluctantly followed him, the right road completely blew up! Reverend Rose fell on his knees in the middle of the road, thanked God, and promised to serve Him the rest of his life. When he was demobilized, he went to Oxford and became a minister." Jeffrey hardly took a breath. "I invited Reverend Rose to come home to tea with us!"

"Did you ask your mother?" I worried that his enthusiasm could get him into trouble.

"Sure, I did! And she said it would be first rate. Too bad Graham isn't here to meet him."

Reverend Rose came the next week. I had baked scones for the occasion. When I ushered the stately gentleman inside, I introduced myself, "I'm Milly Halliday, Mrs. Mason's help.

"Jeffrey thinks very highly of you. You are a big part of the reason that he became a Christian. Now we need to agree that his mother will become a Christian."

"Yes, I long for that day."

"The Bible says where two or three agree as touching anything, it will be done for them."

I heard Mrs. Mason come in from the backyard as we shook hands in agreement. I returned to the kitchen to finish preparing the tea.

Reverend Rose visited frequently after that, always arriving with a rose in his hand for me, and saying, "I came for those delicious scones of yours!"

One memorable evening, Mrs. Mason made an appointment to see Reverend Rose in his office. Two hours later she returned with a radiant face. "I've done it, Milly. I've done it!"

"Done what, Mrs. Mason?"

"Why, I've forgiven my husband! And tomorrow I shall call him up and tell him so. I went to Reverend Rose to talk about my problems, and he said that what I needed was Christ in my life. I needed to be cleansed and forgiven of my past, so I could start anew. I had to forgive, so that I could be forgiven." As she spoke, she opened the wine cupboard, pulled the bottles out, and emptied them down the sink. She threw two sets of playing cards into the trash. Awestruck, I followed her to the piano, where she played my choir hymns with gusto.

"I always wanted to play those with meaning."

Mrs. Mason was a new woman. She called Graham and invited him to return home. However, since he was involved with his classes and friends, he decided to continue to stay at the boarding school.

During a Sunday afternoon visit with my parents, I shared with my mother the changes in Mrs. Mason. "We pray together about everything."

"I know someone you should pray for, Milly."

"Who's that, Mummy?"

"Eddie Ware. He's joined the air force." I had not seen him in months, and it surprised me. "He applied last week," she continued.

"Have you seen him since?"

"No, they sent him to boot camp immediately."

I had many things to pray about the next week. Mrs. Mason added another one. She began attending the Church of England where Reverend Rose ministered.

"Milly, would you come to church with me? I would feel more comfortable going with someone."

At first, I was hesitant, but after attending services a few times, I concluded that the vicar, Reverend Rose, loved God and taught a vital Christianity. Also, Jeffrey and I participated in their youth activities. Reverend Rose taught that there are four absolutes in a Christian's life: absolute love, absolute unselfishness, absolute purity, and absolute honesty. This intrigued me, since from all that I could observe, he lived by them.

During our youth get-togethers, he stood and asked: "All right. Anyone have any problems this week?"

On one occasion, a girl who worked at a flower shop confided: "Well, I've been saying that flowers are fresh to the customers in the store where I work, because that's what the boss told me to say, but they're not fresh."

Reverend Rose said, "You can't lie. If he insists you tell untruths, then you have to leave the job."

She came back the next week to report: "The owner said that I had to cover for him and say the flowers were fresh, so I quit. The next day, I got a new job, and it's

ALL SAINTS
SANDERSTEAD

much better." I sat enthralled. *God stands by those who obey His Word,* I thought.

On Saturday mornings, the youth of the church gathered at the rectory to play tennis and walk together. After a full day of activity, we had a "quiet time" in the evening. We sat in a silent circle and each invited God to speak to us. With pencil and paper in hand, we wrote down what the Lord said. After a half-hour of silence, the service was opened for us to share what we felt the Lord had told us. Sometimes we confessed our weaknesses and faults and asked for help. Other times we gave testimonies of what God had done for us that week. We also prayed for one another and were encouraged to write letters to each other, if we chose to during the week.

The nations, not having Reverend Rose for their leader, heated up with hatred and talked of war.

Since Mrs. Mason had found personal peace, the impending war news did not bother her. It was business as usual, making new Christian friends, and enjoying each other's fellowship.

A particularly close friend was Dr. Lenanten, a lady physician. One Sunday morning, I sat beside her in church, since Mrs. Mason had gone to spend the weekend at school with Graham.

The weekly announcements were read: Mrs. Gower had pneumonia and needed prayer; the youth group were going on a picnic the following Saturday morning and everyone was to bring a sack lunch; choir practice was going to be an hour earlier.

The choir then stood up and sang a rousing rendition of *To God be the Glory*, which set the atmosphere for one of Reverend Rose's challenging sermons. He had walked up to the podium and opened his Bible when a deacon, looking pale and somewhat embarrassed, appeared by Reverend Rose's side and whispered to him.

All of the color drained from the minister's face. He turned to us and announced, "We are at war. Let us pray." There was a gasp from the congregation, and we all bowed our heads. His prayer was fervent, "Oh, God, help our country in this hour. Give our leaders wisdom. Grant our soldiers courage. Please keep each one of us in the center of Your will, supporting each other with prayer. Use us for your honor and glory." As soon as he said amen, he dismissed the service.

Dr. Lenanten, a sedate woman in her fifties, jumped up from our pew, grabbed my arm and pulled me through the crowd to her car.

"Hurry, Milly," she panted. Her hat, unused to its owner's whirlwind of activity, had slipped to the side of her head.

"Bombs could fall any minute!" As soon as the doors of the vehicle closed, she revved the engine and drove as if pursued by hornets.

Contrary to Dr. Lenanten's fears, bombs did not fall for many months. However, during the days that followed, everyone prepared for the impending bombing. Gas masks were issued to everyone. We were required to carry them everywhere we went. Special alarm sirens were installed in each neighborhood, and their signal system was taught. The consensus was we must band together and win this war. We must do our little part in the body of mankind to destroy the pathogen that threatened our civilization.

During this time, my sister Ruth married a wonderful man named Howard Mash, and a year later gave birth to a baby boy, David. I tried to go to their home as often as I could.

One November afternoon, I visited Ruth and played with the baby. As he sat in his bath water, I remarked, "Oh, Ruth, he is so precious! Listen to him coo! It sounds like music!" He then gurgled and splashed the water with his little fists.

"If you watch him, Milly, I'll get you another cup of tea," she volunteered as I tickled baby David's foot.

"No more tea, Ruth, thank you. I've got to get back to Mrs. Mason's."

Just then the neighborhood siren sounded. We had been taught to listen for several different sounds. One blast meant for us to put on gas masks. Completely taken by surprise, we looked at each other, speechless for a second. Then I shouted, "Oh, Ruth! That one blast means we're going to get bombed!"

She grabbed David and ran to get her gas mask. Since mine was beside my purse, I snatched it and followed her to the cupboard under the stairs. The siren wailed forlornly as we squeezed into the tight space. David sensed our fear and began to cry. Suddenly, accompanying the noise, I heard a shrill whistle.

"What's that?" I asked.

"That's the whistle guard," she shouted over David's screams. "He's supposed to walk around the neighborhood and be sure everyone has found protection."

"What about *his* protection?"

Before Ruth had time to answer, we heard thunder-like crashes. We started to pray for ourselves, for our loved ones in the other parts of the city, and for the whistle guard. As moments went by in a nightmare of shrieks and crashes, we were able to distinguish between the booms of the anti-aircraft guns and the rumble of the enemy's planes and bombs. *Ding! Ping!* We heard shrapnel rain down on our roof when a big shell burst above our area.

The bomb must be right over us, I thought as the house shook. Then a hymn came to my mind, *Safe in the Arms of Jesus*. I was at peace wondering which breath would be our last.

An hour later, the siren began to blow a steady pitch. It was an "all clear." The enemy had done its damage and was gone.

However, at first our legs refused to move from their cramped position. David clung to Ruth as we walked through the house and outdoors surveying the damage. We watched burning paper fall from the sky and cinders float through the air. A huge clean-up job was now all around us.

"Oh, Ruth! I hope Mummy and Daddy are all right." I was so concerned about them that I made a special trip to see them on Sunday.

I found everyone fine and busy. Gladys was at work in a hospital; Elsie was a cook for the fire brigade; Grace was occupied with Mrs. Darby, who had developed a heart problem and needed constant care.

My brother, John, was employed at the airport. He explained that his group was being evacuated to Wales. "Milly," he asked, "will you come with me to look at the airport damage?"

A walk with him meant that I would miss church, but I agreed, "Sure, let's go. We might not get another chance to be together for a while."

We walked the two miles to the airport, enjoying our time alone to share with each other.

"Oh, Johnny, look!" I gasped in horror as I surveyed what had once been an airport.

"Terrible! Imagine if I had been here." Johnny's eyes widened. "Look, over there! I used to work on the top floor of that gutted building."

Farther ahead, a tank was rolling toward us. A man shouted from the turret, "Find shelter! The Germans are coming!" We looked up and saw a gray cloud of planes in the distance. "Run! Run!"

We grabbed hands and ran for our lives, reaching town, just as full churches emptied into the street. A bus had stopped, and we pushed our way into it with the crowd. The driver revved the engine and screeched onto the road. We climbed the bus stairs to the top open deck to watch breathlessly as the planes bore down. Soon they were overhead. A child peered out from a shelter along the road. He was a neighbor boy. Later that day, I heard he had been killed, his head severed from his body when a bomb hit right above him.

Suddenly, the bus shook from the explosion of a bomb. The driver stopped the bus. "Everyone out! I can't go any farther!"

The fumes, acrid dust, and smoke blocked our visibility to know where to run, but miraculously, we found our way into an air raid shelter. I trembled uncontrollably and told Johnny, "I won't ever miss another Sunday service!"

Following this Sunday afternoon close call, Mrs. Mason and I spent many nights under the dining table with the piano to the side of us. "Oh, Mrs. Mason, how long will this awful war last?"

"I don't know, Milly, but I'm certainly glad to have peace in my soul, even though there is chaos around me." She was smiling, and I agreed that there was more than one kind of war.

Within a few months, I received notice from the government that I must be actively involved in the war effort. A housemaid for the wealthy was not considered essential. Of course, Mrs. Mason was very upset, but the government notice was clear.

"What shall I do, Reverend Rose?" I asked.

"Well, Milly, have you ever had any desires to do anything besides housekeeping?"

I thought a moment. "Yes, ever since Mummy gave birth to my brother Johnny with that alcoholic midwife, I have dreamed of what help a good nurse could be."

"Nursing would be something that the government would agree to, I'm sure," he confirmed.

"But how do I know it's what God wants me to do?" I asked.

"God puts desires in our hearts, Milly, and as long as they are not contrary to His Word, we can proceed, and if it is truly His will, He will work out the details."

Before many days passed, I was packed and moved to Redhill Hospital, ready to start my first year of nurse's training.

JOINS THE ROYAL AIR FORCE, 1938-1940

M y first assignment in the Royal Air Force was boot camp. Six weeks of shooting, marching, and saluting. The second assignment was technical school where I became an airplane mechanic and fitter. At the end of the course, each man was given an assignment to fabricate objects entirely by hand. We were required to fit complicated shapes like a puzzle to a thousandth of an inch.

The day after the final exam, I entered the lunchroom and overheard two instructors in a heated conversation, "He's better than you are!"

"Oh, no, he isn't! Ware's good, but I'm his teacher, and I'm best!"

"His is better than you, and that's all I can say," the first one stated flatly. I decided it was best to leave quickly.

Back at the dorm, I met with one of my new friends, Brian With. He was a Christian, and we often attended church services together. However, new movies were consistently shown on Sundays during chapel times. Sometimes, I chose entertainment instead of the religious meeting. On the other hand, Brian never missed a chapel service, and he also prayed on his knees by his bed in the barracks morning and night. Sometimes men threw their boots at him, and they all heckled and ridiculed him unmercifully.

"With, why do you put up with it? You could pray in your bunk, and they'd leave you alone!" I suggested.

With was quiet for a few seconds, then said, "Jesus went to the cross for me, this is the least I can do for Him." As I still looked concerned he patted me on the back, "Don't worry about me, Ware. I've got tough skin."

Often men joked, "Where's Ware?"

"He's with With," and they laughed.

On the same day I overheard my instructor speak about me, I reached the barracks at the same time as With, who had just come off of duty. "In the lunch room they were discussing who's the best mechanic," I told him as I hung up my jacket.

"And everyone said that it was you, right?" He looked at me with a grin.

"No, not everyone. The instructor angrily protested that, of course, since he was my teacher, he was better. I'm concerned about where this might lead."

"Sort of like King Saul and David in the Bible. Saul got upset that everyone in Israel thought more of David, a mere shepherd, than he, the king."

With used his Bible to describe most events. Quoting from the Bible was difficult for most of the people around us to understand, but I enjoyed it.

"I guess you're right. I think I'll have to stay out of his path as much as possible."

From that day on, the instructor was unreasonable. He graded me severely and caused me to miss the elite mechanic group status. I was very upset.

"It just isn't fair, With!" I complained bitterly to my friend.

"All things work together for good, Ware. God may be working something out that you know nothing about."

"Yeah," I muttered, "maybe you're right, but I still feel cheated."

After the schooling, we were given orders and sent to bases around the country.

"With, I'm going to miss you. You have my respect and admiration, and I hope all goes well with you."

"Ware, I've appreciated your being my friend when others threw things at me. I won't forget it." He shook my hand heartily.

I was sent to a squadron that had been in the air force for years. "Well, look what we've got here!" a tough old airman harassed me as we headed to the airplanes we were to service. "A mere baby! Did your mum untie your apron strings yet?"

"Did Mumsy send you off with a clean hankie?" another man chimed in.

"I hope you don't expect us to wipe your nose for you. This squadron is known for how tough we are, and we don't take kindly to being sent infants that need diapering," another sneered.

I ignored their jabs. *I'll show them what I can do,* I thought. But no matter how hard I worked, it only seemed to annoy them.

A year after I joined the air force, war was declared, and our squadron was told: "Pack up and put into storage all of your personal things. You are being sent to France."

We were issued rifles and fifty rounds of ammunition. Very concerned about the order, I wondered if we were being sent to the front lines to be foot soldiers.

"Goin' to cry, Ware?" one of the men teased. "Maybe you should go home to Mummy!"

I turned away from my tormentor. With such mates, who needed enemies?

We arrived in France by ship and were driven to Epernay, in the north, then were ordered to clear land and set up an airfield to receive and service airplanes. Since we expected any minute to have to fight the Germans, the entire squadron worked hard and had the job done quickly. Warfare was stalled for nine months, however, as Germany held the Siegfried Line, and France, the Maginot.

After the airfield was set up, our days began at 6:30 A.M. I was assigned to play the wake-up call on my trumpet. Following wake-up, we went to the mess hall for breakfast.

"Little Boy Blue played his horn well this morning, didn't he?" one of the squadron said as I passed his table.

"I don't know which I hate worse, his lousy playing, or waking up," his mate added.

After breakfast we exercised, practiced our duties, and, ever alert for the sound of aircraft, rotated guard duty.

One warm morning, I sat alone in the guard shack. The breeze brought in a bee that buzzed around the room, but not locating nectar, flew out again. War seemed far away as my eyes took in the vineyards as far as my eyes could see that surrounded the airfield. I glanced toward the roof of a farm cottage where I had been invited to share last night's supper. A cute mademoiselle also was there. Neither of us had understood the other's native language, but sparks had flown between us, anyway.

I was distracted by another buzzing sound, an airplane. Jolted into the present, I remembered that I was to meet the aircraft as it landed. Since the closest route to the airfield was over the roof of the guard shack, I climbed up the wall and stepped gingerly onto the shingles. The brittle roofing disintegrated, and I crashed through to the floor. Pain shot through my foot.

"The baby's done got himself hurt," were the words of comfort I received from those that found me. The officer in charge sent me in a truck to the closest field hospital where they diagnosed my broken foot. The bottom half of my leg was then bandaged in a cast.

With my foot propped up, I sat on a cot and read or visited with the other patients.

One morning, a new doctor made the rounds with the nursing staff. Each of us was required, if able, to stand at attention at the foot of his cot. As I stood, assisted by a crutch, I watched the doctor approach. He wore jackboots and jaspers, not exactly part of a British uniform.

"What's the matter with you?" he looked me up and down. A nurse behind him read my diagnosis from her chart; then he snapped, "Can you walk?"

"Well, yes. It hurts, but I can walk," I said.

"Lie down," he ordered and yanked the leg cast off. I wondered whose side in the war he was on.

"Get up!" he demanded. The cast lay in bits at the foot of the bed. "Walk!"

I began to take small, painful steps. Within a few days, I was fine. He knew what he was doing.

Before being sent back to my squadron, I went to see the officer in charge.

"Sir, please send me to a different squadron."

"Why do you want to change squadrons, airman?"

"I'm not happy there, sir. I could do a better job with a different group of men."

"An unusual request. I'll send you to another, but I'd better not hear any complaints about you. Try to make the best of every situation, airman."

"Yes, sir. Thank you, sir!"

My new squadron leader was an Australian named Jim Lease. He was jolly and always seemed to have his soldiers' interests at heart. Under his leadership, some of us were sent to the south of France, where we practiced aerial bomb drops on rowboats in the Mediterranean. We also flew over temporary camps for thousands of refugees from the Spanish Revolution. We waved at them, and they were friendly as they waved back to us.

Sometimes we slept in beautiful French mansions with tall windows. The rooms, stripped of furniture, carpets and paintings, caused our boots and voices to echo throughout the big rooms. Most of the time, though, we stayed in rough farm huts with crude outhouses and straw-strewn dirt floors.

One day my squadron returned from the airfield to the village. "What in the world is that stench?" a soldier asked.

The indescribably awful odor hung over the whole area. "What a filthy, vile smell!" he continued. I agreed as we trudged together to the mess hall.

We lined up and were handed plates of Limberger cheese. Instantly, we knew where the foul odor came from.

"What is this smelly stuff?" someone asked. We were aghast to think that we were expected to eat it. As hungry as we were, we could hardly bear the odor. After I cut the hunk of cheese, I noticed the odor lingered on my knife. Even when I buried the knife and later resurrected it, the odor remained!

During our off hours, we visited French bistros, drank wine, and enjoyed greeting the French mademoiselles. Also during our recreation times, we British soldiers sang and whistled ribald songs. Thomas, an especially gifted singer, was always called to "give us a song!" His father was one of the best comedians of London, whom I had heard sing and perform pantomimes before the war.

Some men visited the red-light districts and encouraged me to join them. "Come on, Ware! You don't know what you're missing!"

I might not, but I do know I'm not getting diseases that are in those places, I told myself.

When the men were headed in that direction, I looked for other things to do. Sometimes I remembered With and felt guilty about not going to chapel services. It was rare to find a good chaplain. Most of them served solely as social workers.

One day, at mess hall, I looked up to see Goff, an old friend from the Coulsdon Sunday afternoon Bible class.

"Goff! A vision from home! Come sit here!" We recounted what had happened to us through the last year, where we'd gone, and what we'd done. Then Goff asked, "What's the chaplain like here?"

"Well, I can't say as I know, but we can find out."

We attended a service together and found the chaplain to be quite good. He warned us, "In every person there are two fires, a wild fire that gets fueled by worldly, evil things, which can engulf and destroy; and the hearth of our heart. If we read the Bible and pray, our hearts get warm and soft enough to help those around us. It all comes down to which fire gets fueled."

I realized that I needed to extinguish some wild fires in my life and prayed, "Oh, God, it's not easy to be a Christian. I do love You and ask for You to keep me and help me."

June of 1939 saw the German forces march around the Maginot and Siegfried lines. They invaded Belgium and then France. Suddenly, we did not have enough hours in the day. Every airplane had a logbook, and we had certain planes that each of us was responsible to service. Many aircraft that we sent off never returned; some came back in with engines dangling off of the wing or propellers missing.

When our airplanes were parked on the airfield, we mechanics had to stay beside them, ready to spring into action and start the engine when the alarm sounded. The pilots in their quarters heard the same alarm and immediately dressed, put on parachutes, and ran to their aircraft. By the time they reached us, the plane was ready to fly. They jumped into their cockpit, while we helped strap them in.

"Good luck," we murmured, "come back soon."

British troops coined a phrase, "Joe for King!" which represented the common soldier's frustration with war.

Our monarch, King George, represented all that we were fighting for in the war. To speak irreverently of him in this time of national crisis was severely frowned upon.

"Joe" was the name of the ruthless dictator of the Soviet Union, Joseph Stalin, who starved millions of peasants who opposed him. To refer to this inhumane dictator as our king, even in jest, was risking severe punishment.

It was not in jest, however, but in extreme frustration, that I uttered the unspeakable words and risked my air force career. I was trying to start a twin engine plane. The pilot was already in the cockpit with the window open, waiting for me. I had turned the crank so many times that I was breathless. Exhausted, I panted, "Oh, Joe for King!"

The pilot stuck his head out of the window and said, "What was that?"

My heart froze within me. I had just said something that could put me in the brig.

"Just a figure of speech, sir," I said weakly, and cranked with all of my might. I thought I heard him laugh. As he took off, he waved, which I hoped meant that he did not hold my outburst against me.

"What's That?"

"Just a Figure of Speech, Sir!"

Of the original group of mechanics that I trained with, I learned that none of them returned home alive. When I heard this, I considered my friend With's words: "'All things work together for good'; God may be working something out that you know nothing about." I grieved over the loss of my companions' lives and wondered why God had saved mine.

We also lost our much-loved Officer Lease, who died in a plane wreck. Another valuable life snuffed out. As the war got hotter, we witnessed line after line of weary and injured soldiers returning from the front lines. If there is any glory in war, it was not seen in the defeated, miserable faces that we saw pass through our airfield each day.

One morning I woke up nauseated. My stomach hurt, and when I stood, it hurt much worse. I dragged myself to the infirmary, where a nurse took my temperature and helped me to a chair. A doctor checked me.

"Appendicitis," was his diagnosis.

I was put onto a truck and driven to a field hospital in another town, where I waited all day for attention. The doctors were extremely busy with the injured coming in from the front lines. In the evening, a doctor came through the ward and stopped in front of me, glanced down at the chart, then back at me. "What's that doing there?" he asked of the little kidney basin that sat by my bedside.

The nurse responded, "He felt sick, sir. It's there in case he vomits."

"Get him to the operating room immediately. His appendix may have burst."

The nurses moved quickly, and the next thing I remember is pain. I moaned and was surprised that a nurse came immediately over to see me. She said brightly, "Hello, soldier. I see you've decided to wake up." She pulled the sheet down from my waist, and to my horror, I saw a big pipe sticking out of my stomach.

"What's that!" I quailed.

"Nothing to worry about. Your appendix ruptured, and this is the drain." Then she rushed off.

"What's her hurry?" I asked the man next to me.

"I think there are more patients than she has time for. I just came from the front and the casualties are enormous. All British troops are in retreat."

I was in the hospital for a few days; then all patients were transferred to trucks, taking us to boats headed for England. I found myself next to men with stumps for legs and arms. Some had bandages across their heads and faces. I lay quietly and thought deeply about life and death and war. How easily our candle can be snuffed out. I learned later that my squadron had been ordered to bomb the river Meuse, to halt the advance of the German invasion. Every one of our planes was wiped out with all of our support crews literally running for their lives. Sadly, some very dear friends of mine were killed, including Thomas, the man with the golden voice.

In England, I was sent to a hospital to recuperate. One of the nurses, Nelly, became quite fond of me. We went for walks and talked.

"Nelly, when I was a child, I was taught that people went to hospitals to die and that all nurses were wicked."

"So what do you think now?"

"The opposite. Nurses are giving, dedicated people."

"Thank you," she smiled.

"Edward, I wonder where you'll be sent when you get better?"

"I don't know. Not back to France. Everyone who was still alive came back at Dunkirk," I said.

"My father sent our family's row boat on that rescue," she said. "I thought that it was stupid, as the channel is a rough piece of water to cross, and I was sure our little boat would sink. But it didn't. It rescued five men!"

"I believe God did a miracle. Fog covered the operation, so the Germans couldn't see what was going on; and the water was totally smooth, so the men were able to be rescued from the beaches."

We walked on in silence as we contemplated the wonder of it. I enjoyed Nelly's friendship but was intimidated by her being an officer. She would have been reprimanded if caught socializing with me, an airman.

A few weeks later, I was sent home where it was a delight to relax and be catered to by my mother. My father continued at his job in London; my sister Joan worked at the American Embassy as a telephone operator; and my brother Cliff was in the navy on a carrier.

After I recovered fully, I received orders to report to the Night Fighters, a squadron whose planes went on night missions. Radar, called IFF (Identification, Friend or Foe) was new at this time. It was so secretive that none of us really knew what it was all about. Curiously, an extra seat was installed in the cockpit for an observer who gazed into a little tube to identify aircraft. At the same time, we were issued carrots to eat, as many carrots as we could consume. The pilots continually munched on carrots. The idea was to mislead "Jerry," to conclude our extraordinary eyesight came from the vitamin A in carrots! Of course, the deception was soon discovered, and the enemy learned that we were using radar.

For a diversion from the sadness of war, I pulled together a few friends to make a bit of money on the side. We formed a band and played for dances on Sunday evenings. We often went to pubs and enjoyed our camaraderie away from the dull barracks. Officers set rank aside and also joined us there, as well as American service men.

The American troops ate better food, had nicer uniforms, and made more money than we did. We resented it, especially when our English girls favored them. But the Americans had their own problems. When they got drunk, they often exhibited their racial prejudices, which resulted in nasty fights and brawls.

Shortly after, Germany started a heavy Luftwaffe air raid on England, beginning the Battle of Britain. Women and children were evacuated from London and other large cities, and blackouts were enforced. London was the prime target. Fifty bombers, escorted by more than a hundred fighters, smashed the capital.

Our squadron also was often bombed. Many of our men were killed, war planes destroyed, and the hangars blown to smithereens. It was a horrific time. Our nerves were stretched to the limit as we stayed up night after night, attending airplanes. Often struck with terror, I stood at my post of duty and watched the enemy's planes come in. I wondered, *Is this going to be it? Is this the end?* I dived to the ground and covered my ears with my hands as the whine of bomb after bomb screeched its way to earth. The bombs pulverized whatever they hit. Anyone within forty to fifty feet of a bomb's detonation was killed or maimed by the shrapnel. Sometimes I felt the powerful blast of wind that accompanied a close hit. The roar of anti-aircraft guns and the screams of the injured created a living hell that I longed to escape.

Becomes a Nurse, 1941–1945

"Hello, Halliday, I'm Nurse Kairns." A student nurse with the telltale navy senior belt read my name badge and greeted me in the lunch room line. It was my first day in nurses' training at Redhill Hospital. I was frightened to be away from all that was familiar, yet awed by the senior status of the nurse speaking to me. I hardly had time to acknowledge her greeting before she asked, "How are things going for you thus far?"

"This morning we had our first class," I said.

"Bed pans, right?"

I warmed up to her immediately. "I'm sure I can handle the bedpans, but I'm a little nervous about what will follow. I passed the emergency entry on my way here and saw a man covered with blood from a large head wound. It scared me to think that some day I'll have to admit someone in his condition."

"You'll have to deal with worse things than that because of this war. If I weren't a Christian, I would have quit before now."

"I'm a Christian too!"

By this time we had been served our food, and Nurse Kairns was called by some of her classmates to sit with them.

"Well, Halliday, keep your chin up. How about stopping by my room this evening? I've got half an hour free before going on night duty, and we can talk a little more. Room number twelve."

"Thank you. I'll be there!" I found a table, and bowed my head in genuine gratitude for the food and for the friendly welcome. The rest of the day went easier, since I had the evening to look forward to.

That night I timidly knocked on the door of room twelve. Nurse Kairns opened the door with a mouth full of bobby pins. She was pinning her nursing cap onto her hair.

"Excuse me," she mumbled through the pins as she ushered me into her room. "I must be off in fifteen minutes. I have to see the head nurse before reporting for duty, but thanks for coming."

"Thank you."

"To put what I have to say bluntly and quickly, I believe in living the Christian life, not talking about it." She waited for me to react. I nodded. "A nurse started with me three years ago. She continually told people that she was a Christian and that they should be, too. For a long time, I felt guilty that I was not bold enough to do that. Then last year she got involved with a Canadian soldier, got pregnant, and ran off with him. It left a bad name for Christianity, since she had been so vocal about her beliefs. I would like to suggest that we meet together every morning at five and pray together before breakfast. Things have become so chaotic with this war that we need each other's Christian strength, so we can have the wisdom to help those in need."

"I would appreciate doing that." I stood to leave. "I'll be here tomorrow morning at five."

"All the best, Halliday. I'm rooting for you," she said and saw me to the door.

Each morning, we met in her room and spent ten minutes in prayer. This helped keep me steady through all the harried experiences of my first year of nursing.

In addition to our daily classes, we performed menial jobs in the hospital. We learned to work, ignoring air raid warning sirens, since there were no shelters.

On one occasion, I went on duty in a ward where every bed sheet was wet with urine. During an air raid, the patients involuntarily urinated in their beds from fear. At that moment, the head nurse walked through the ward with a helmet perched on the top of her nurse's cap. She stopped in front of me as I worked on the beds.

"Nurse, if there is another air raid, run under the bed with the fattest patient. Stay there until it's over. You're no good to us dead."

The possibility of an obese patient landing on me did not carry much appeal. I continued to help the patients, ignoring the air raid sirens.

Another precaution for our well being, each year we nursing students were to fill out a health form. Since my menstrual periods had stopped for a few months, I noted that on the form.

Also, at the end of the first year, all nurses had to pass a written government exam. The day before the exam, I dashed into Kairn's room at five in the morning. "Milly, you look a little pale. Are you feeling all right?"

"Not really. I haven't been eating much but feel heavy, and I'm exhausted. I can't wait to get these exams over and take my holiday!" My mother and I planned to take a train trip to her sister Ada's for a week's vacation.

"Maybe you should sleep a few extra minutes each morning instead of coming to my room," she suggested.

"Oh, Kairns! Please! That's what has kept me going! No, I'll get past this exam, take my week off, and then I'll feel better."

The following morning, when I entered the somber exam room, I began to feel light-headed. The room whirled once, then everything went black. The next thing I heard were doctors' voices discussing my condition with matron, the head of the nurses. "Well, obviously, this girl is pregnant."

"No! Not Halliday, Doctor," she remonstrated.

By this time, my head was clear. "Absolutely not, Doctor!" I voiced clearly.

"That's what they all say, Nurse." He turned away coldly and indifferently.

I struggled to sit up, but since I felt faint again, I laid back down.

"Now, now, Halliday. Lie still, and we'll get to the bottom of this. This happens to many girls as the doctor said, although you are the last one I would have expected. If you've made a mistake, just come clear with it."

I started to cry. "Matron, it would have to be like Jesus and Mary if I were, because I have never known a man."

They all left the room, and I sobbed until my pillow was wet. Since every time I tried to sit up, I felt faint, I couldn't leave my bed.

In the meantime, Matron called my mother to cancel our vacation.

To my relief, another doctor came to examine me and asked me many specific questions. He became alarmed as I answered them, and called the nurse in charge.

"This is a life threatening case. She must be operated on tomorrow morning."

He stepped outside of the room, but I could hear his report to Matron, "Sister, this young woman is likely not to be alive tomorrow. She has tumors on her ovaries. Make her comfortable, and we'll do all we can, but I make no promises."

Visitors and flowers arrived right away. My friend, Dr. Lenanten, heard that the original doctor in charge had falsely accused me of being pregnant. She was furious. I don't know what she said to him, but before I was wheeled into the operating room, he came in to see me and apologized.

"It happens so often now that girls get pregnant, Nurse, that I just made a mistake. I am sorry."

Matron came in to see me. "Halliday, is there anything I can do for you, anything at all?" I remembered Kairns and her desire for a prayer time.

"I would like permission to have a Christian meeting each week somewhere in the nurses' quarters."

"You shall have it, Nurse. Just come through this, and you shall have it," she said.

Reverend Rose came in and prayed for me. He reminded me of Romans 8:28, "All things," and he repeated, "*all things*, work together for good to them that love God, to them who are the called according to His purpose."

"I know, Reverend Rose, and I am not afraid," I assured him. "The only thing that bothers me is that I missed the first year exam and will have to wait a whole year to be able to take it again."

"Ah, Milly, I know that it is difficult to understand why this happened, but God is mindful, and although we don't understand right now, there is a purpose in it. The Bible says that God knows when the sparrows fall, and that He knows the number of hairs on our head, so be assured that He knows and cares about all of your worries and frustrations. Just give

God thanks, if you can, as He said in First Thessalonians 5:18. 'In everything give thanks for this is the will of God in Christ Jesus concerning you.' His will is perfect. 'All things work together for good.' Rest on His promises."

The anesthesiologist for my operation was an acquaintance I had met the week before at a bus stop. "I owe you for that bus fare you loaned me, Halliday. Here it is. I don't want to have to put it on your coffin." As he placed the coins in my hand, I wondered what use I'd have for them. It was ironic. If I had been going on vacation with my mother, I would have found the coins useful, but my hospital gown didn't even have pockets!

To everyone's surprise, I survived the operation, but awoke in terrible pain. "You've had major surgery, Halliday, and it will be a while before you're back to yourself."

As I lay in the recovery room, I remembered all of the "appropriate words" I had used to communicate with my patients. From this perspective, they sounded meaningless.

With a worried frown, the doctor entered my room. "There were three large growths attached to your ovaries, Halliday. The good news is that they were not malignant, and we were able to remove them before they burst. The bad news is that you will probably not be able to have children."

"That's all right, Doctor. I don't even plan on getting married."

I was assigned a special nurse who read to me to divert my mind from terrible gas pain. "I have chosen *The Wind in the Willows* to read to you," she said, opening the book.

"The title sure is appropriate!" I volunteered. We both started to laugh, but the excruciating pain that shot through me brought tears to my eyes.

The nurse grabbed a pillow and put it over my abdomen. "Whenever you cough or laugh, it will help if you hold this over the incision."

"That hurt so bad, I might never laugh again!"

"But to prevent pneumonia you're going to have to cough! Take deep breaths. Fill your lungs slowly, then empty them fully as often as you think about it. With any pain, breathing is a key to relief," she said. "It will also prevent pneumonia. From the amount of flowers and visitors you're getting, it would make a great deal of people sad if you didn't get well. There's a poem that says, 'This, too, shall pass.' Just keep remembering that you're going to get past this!"

After a couple of weeks, I started to feel better. The head matron came into my room and sat next to me. "You know, Nurse, I'm going to be able to use your special skills after this. You have suffered, and I will be able to put you with patients who are suffering. You will be able to understand their needs better than anyone."

I smiled at her and thought of First Corinthians 1:4 . . . *"that we may be able to comfort them which are in any trouble, by the comfort wherewith we ourselves are comforted of God"*.

"In a few days you will be going down to Hazelmere, to the Edith Cavell Nursing Home, where I want you to rest and recuperate," Matron continued. "You will take the train, and in a month or so, you may return and get back to work." She got up to leave, then turned back. "You may start up that nurses' meeting when you get back."

Thrilled to be alive, I waved from the train window to my friends. I was greeted at the Hazelmere train depot by a cluster of retired nurses. "Don't walk so fast, Halliday. Take it easy. Let me do that for you, Halliday." Every one of the retired nurses attempted to revive all of their nursing skills and focus on me, their only patient.

A month later, I returned to nurse's training and joined the first-year class again. Matron kept her promise and provided a room with a piano and songbooks. One of the new girls played the piano as we gathered on a weekly basis to hear various Christian speakers and to sing and pray.

Periodically, the nursing school sponsored a dance, inviting military officers from the area. We Christians did not attend but watched in amazement from our windows at the vulgar behavior of our fellow students. During each event, a knock came on the door where we were gathered.

"Ladies, Matron requests that you come down."

"All right. Thank you." Obediently, we went down to the dance, greeted Matron, and returned to our rooms upstairs. We were not interested in fraternizing with military officers whom we did not know.

However, on one occasion, a nurse came to me in the hospital corridor. "Halliday, there is a handsome young Egyptian doctor who wishes to meet you."

"Sorry, no interest. Tell him I'm too busy," I said as I shifted patient charts from one arm to the other.

"But he knows that you can't be any busier than we are. Any one of us would find time! I bet if you did go with him, you would get kissed."

"Nobody's going to kiss me," I assured her.

"He's so handsome, you wouldn't be able to resist!" She teased.

"Tell him I'll go for a walk by the lake with him this evening, and I'll prove to you that he won't kiss me."

That evening I did not feel confident. I wondered why I had fallen for the bait? I fell on my knees and prayed, "Lord, I should not have been so gullible. I'm sorry. I'm not worried that I'll get kissed, but that it is a foolish, unnecessary errand." Just then someone knocked on the door.

"Guest in the waiting room for you, Halliday."

I ran downstairs and greeted a truly handsome young man.

"Thank you so much for your time, Miss Halliday," he said and shook my hand. "Do you need a coat?"

"No, I will be fine without one, thank you." And we proceeded to the pathway that led to the lake.

"I am told that you are from Egypt. Would you please tell me about your country? I am interested in hearing about it."

"Most of my country is desert, but where I live is the most beautiful spot in the world, the Nile Delta. I left four years ago to study in England, and now I am homesick for my country and my father and mother." We sat on the grass and watched the moonlight reflect off the lake.

"Do you have brothers and sisters?" I asked.

He then described his family, his life with them, and also a glimpse of the culture of Egypt. Suddenly, when I glanced at my watch, I realized that more than an hour had passed.

"Thank you so much for the lovely time, but I must return to the dorm now," I said and got up.

"You have allowed me a visit home without having to travel there." He looked at me gratefully. On the way to the dorm, we discussed the war and our part in it.

At the entrance to the dorm, he shook my hand again, and I entered the nurses' quarters. As soon as the front door closed, I was surrounded. "All right, Halliday. What was his kiss like?"

"He didn't kiss me," I said as I headed for my room.

"What an old fuddy-duddy. Nothing but a cold potato. Spoil sport!"

The matron realized that repeating the first year's course work might bore me, so she kept me occupied with her special patients. At the end of the year, I took the First Year Government Exam, passed it, and proceeded to the next level.

Our nursing routine was very rigorous. Each day we worked long hours and often double shifts.

On one occasion, I was the night nurse in a women's geriatric ward. The bombs dropped all night, shaking the buildings with their explosions. We could feel the walls being sucked in and out from the pressure of those explosions. The old people cried, screamed, and begged for attention. I couldn't keep up with the wet beds, and when morning came, I determined that I would not leave the ward until every patient was dry, and also calmed and reassured.

When the morning nurse came on duty, she reminded me, "Halliday, Florence Nightingale died years ago. You're not to worry about these beds."

"These dear old folk deserve a clean bed," I insisted.

"It'll be taken care of. Now report to your dorm. You need some sleep."

Another night, a bomb dropped on a mansion that housed Canadian soldiers. Shortly after, the hospital halls were filled with those soldiers, slashed by the slivered glass. One young man with deep cuts on his back cried like a baby. He wanted someone to give him comfort. My heart went out to him, but I couldn't respond. There were so many who urgently needed our help. We only had time for the critically wounded, requiring immediate attention, such as stopping the flow of blood. We were also carefully following the supervising doctor's orders.

Often we were called upon to go out in the ambulances to pick up people after air raids. There was carnage everywhere. The only way we could cope emotionally was to look at a scene and plan how and what we could do to help.

Once an ambulance brought in a fifty-year-old man who was found naked on the streets. He was incoherent and threateningly swung at anyone who tried to help him. A doctor ordered him to be locked in a small, rubber-padded cell. I was to give him a shot of morphine. Like a lion in a cage, he paced back and forth around the enclosure, then peered through a little glass slot at me. Four staff members held him down as I delivered the injection.

When I learned the next morning that he died of a heart attack, I was devastated. I felt responsible for his death.

Mrs. Mason called me on the telephone that evening, and I shared my feelings with her. "There was no way he deserved that. I feel so guilty. I gave the shot that killed him."

"No, Milly, dear, you were working under doctor's orders. Your shot did not kill him. War killed him."

I hardened myself more and more to the sights and sounds of death. On the gynecology ward, we admitted three botched abortion cases every night. By the time most of the girls reached us, they had nearly hemorrhaged to death. My task was to search through each bloody placenta for the dead baby and drop it into a jar of formaldehyde. All of the staff were disgusted with these abortion victims. They interrupted our critical care and attention for dying bomb victims.

One night, the doctor in charge threw her hand towel down and said in disgust, "I'm not wasting another pint of blood on any of you! You can die! There are dying soldiers on the front lines in need of this blood."

One of these girls, Olive, came in sobbing, "Oh, Nurse, I really wanted the baby, but my parents would have been furious. I thought it was the only thing I could do. I am a Christian, and maybe I have sinned the unpardonable!"

"No, Olive, dear, to kill is not the unpardonable sin. When Jesus was on the cross it says in Luke 23:34 that He forgave those who were killing Him. If you desire to be forgiven, He is waiting to do so."

"I will ask Him," she said, her pale face lined with pain.

Detectives and staff were determined to find the abortionist who was mutilating these girls. They asked me, "Do you think that you could get Olive to tell you who performed her abortion? Each girl is coming in with the same symptoms but refuses to say who did it."

"I will do my best," I responded.

I went to her room. "Olive, you look more at peace." I entered, holding a thermometer.

"Yes, I am forgiven," she whispered.

"Olive, do you want to help others who find themselves pregnant as you did?" I asked.

"Yes, I do. I've been thinking about it. The woman who does the abortions threatens terrible things if we tell, but I must."

She proceeded to describe how the girls were informed of the woman's services, how much she charged, and the procedure she used.

Unexpectedly that night, Olive died from the gruesome mutilation that had been inflicted upon her. But following her death, thanks to her disclosure, the abortionist was caught and jailed. The stream of young victims stopped.

During these hectic days I met a young doctor who shared many of my interests. He came from a wealthy family and wanted to spend his life in medical research. One afternoon on the gynecology ward, he stopped me in the hallway.

"I noticed on the roster that you have tomorrow off. How about coming with me to London? I'll take you to a symphony and to dinner afterwards."

The symphony sounded great, not to mention dinner. We had lived on rations for so long that I had forgotten what real food tasted like. The ration book allowed everyone each month: one egg, one cup of sugar, four ounces of butter, one pound of meat, no fresh fruit, and few desserts.

Our hot drink in the morning was so weak that we could not tell the difference between tea and coffee. However, bread was not rationed, so we filled up on it.

We also had special names for some of the meals: "Tonsillectomy Pie" and "Appendectomy Stew." These meals had tiny pieces of meat in them. We joked that they had come from the surgery room that morning.

Pregnant women were given slightly better rations. On the maternity ward, milk was kept in the refrigerator. One day the milk bottle was missing. A nurse confessed to drinking the milk, then nearly gagged when we told her she had drunk mother's breast milk. Needless to say, she never drank the maternity ward milk again.

The invitation was so tempting, I agreed to go to London with Doctor Reese. The concert was relaxing, although I couldn't help thinking about the needy just outside the building. At the restaurant in Soho, I was delighted to see bananas on the menu as well as other desserts. My date ordered a steak for us that filled our plates. The steak was so large, I had to leave most of mine behind.

"Why didn't you wrap your steak in your napkin and take it home?" My mother lamented, when she heard about my leaving food on my plate. "We're so desperate for meat!"

Shortly following my evening out, I was assigned the tuberculosis ward. The patients, ordered to get as much fresh air as possible when the weather permitted, were placed in chairs or beds on the patios.

Often we could see "doodle bombs" (V-1 unmanned bombs with engines) pass the hospital on their way to London. The air force was determined to shoot them down in the countryside before they hit the populated capitol. We could see the air fights from the hospital windows. One of my patients on ABR (absolute bed rest) would jump up and down on his bed and shout excitedly, "Get him, boy! Get him!" It was impossible to keep him still.

Long hours and continued stress were so tiring that whenever I returned to the dorm I fell asleep, sometimes still in uniform.

One morning, on my way to breakfast, I vividly remembered a dream during the night before. I related it to friends sitting beside me in the cafeteria.

"I was in a coffin going into church. My head was above the coffin, so I could see that the church was full, and the choir was on either side of the aisle. All of you were singing as I went up to the altar!"

The entire table of nurses started to laugh. "Old Halliday is getting married!" they chanted.

"No, I'm not! How can you read that into my dream?"

"When you get married you die to your past life. Even your name changes, and you start a new life!"

An Airman in Canada, 1940-1946

During the Battle of Britain, I received new orders. As I tore them open, my eyes grew wide in disbelief, "Canada!"

The war had caused such havoc in England that the air force couldn't adequately train new airmen. In Canada, there was plenty of room and no danger, so crews, airplanes, ground personnel, and back-up equipment were being sent there.

"Canada!" It still sounded like a dream come true to me as I waited to board the train that was to take me and the other troops to a port in Scotland. I was about to fulfill a childhood dream of crossing the seas when I least expected it. My only sorrow was to leave family behind in a country where death was a daily threat.

We arrived at the port-of-departure and were marched up a gangplank into a huge troop ship. The vessel quickly filled with thousands of men divided into groups of two hundred. Our group was sent below decks, where we were accommodated in numbered hammocks. They hung like dark clouds across a room. Each of us looked earnestly for the hammock where we were to store our equipment and sleep. "I hope we sail soon," I said to the man who claimed the aerial bed next to mine.

"I hope we have a smooth trip. I get seasick," he warned me. I noticed that he looked a little green.

The well-laden boat stopped in Northern Ireland. Then it turned and went back to Scotland, where we stayed in port another week. Apparently the U-boat activity made it unsafe for a single vessel to cross the Atlantic. A fifty-ship convoy gathered to accompany us, including a couple of destroyers and a battle cruiser.

On the upper deck of our ship, separated only by a rope, were several hundred German prisoners. They were primarily pilots who had been shot down over England. Often they stood by the rope and signaled to us to trade with them. Some of the Germans spoke better English than we did, so we understood that they wanted cigarettes.

Every British soldier or airman, whether he wanted it or not, was allocated tobacco. I only smoked a little, so I had a lot to trade. We exchanged for bits and pieces of their uniforms: medals, badges, insignia, and gloves.

Sometimes they stood and sang. The cadence of their music was militaristic and stirred us with its beauty.

Not to be outdone, we responded with: *Roll Out The Barrel* and *Pack Up Your Troubles*, jolly tunes that had no military significance. They laughed at one of our songs, *We're Going to Hang Out the Washing on the Siegfried Line*! They were convinced they would win the war. I'm glad that choral ability was not the criterion for winning the war or they might have!

Aside from cigarettes, we believed that the German prisoners on the ship were treated better than we, the troops, were, because they were officers. There was all the difference in the world between the treatment of enlisted personnel and officers.

"Ware, I was sent on a job to the officer's mess this morning and saw menus, fine china, bread rolls, real meat, wine, and desserts," the man in the hammock next to mine complained one evening. I was amazed that he had noticed since he had been seasick since the day we sailed.

The swill that we soldiers were fed made us furious. In the morning, we were given gray porridge. At noon, a brown, gooey-gook they called stew. At night, yellow curry with little bits of meat afloat in it. Day after day the same fare. We felt that we were being treated as pigs, the only difference being that the slop came on a plate.

At each of our meals, the officer on duty was required to ask, "Any complaints?"

That night I stood up and responded, "Yes!"

As Oliver in Dickens' great novel I raised my plate and asked, "How'd you like to eat this?"

"What's the matter with it?" the officer seemed a little worried.

"Well, taste it." I dared him. "And while you are at it, try this coffee. The cook must have used yesterday's dishwater to make it!"

He took my cup, gritted his teeth, and siphoned a drop into his mouth, "Hmmmmm, not so bad!" then quickly returned it to me.

Each day the injustice and inequality was brought to the attention of the officer on duty. Sometimes the officer nibbled a little bit of our food to pacify us. On one occasion, to emphasize the point, a soldier brought a little human excrement into the dining hall with him, and mixed it with the brown stew on his plate. When the time came to register complaints, he then stood up and asked, "What does this stuff smell like?"

The officer went over and smelled the stew, "Ughhh!" he shouted, and spit. For a few days our rations improved, but then reverted back to the same as before.

Despite our miserable food, we enjoyed the balmy and beautiful weather in the south Atlantic. We reached there within a week. At that point, since we had passed the treacherous part of our voyage, our ship parted company with the convoy. We headed north alone.

After a few days of smooth waters, the weather changed drastically. A hurricane was in our path. Our boat tossed in the waves like a child's toy in the bathtub. I clung to the edges of my hammock and wondered how the ship was able to hold itself together as it shuddered and shook through the onslaught. Men were seasick all around me. Somehow the genes of my ancestors came through, and I was not ill. I thought of my grandfather Suckling and how he had relished his tussles with the sea.

As men groaned and retched around me, I decided I had to get a breath of fresh air. I staggered to the stairs and climbed up to the hatch. We always wore our uniform, and I had on my parade cap. I found it stayed on my head better than my airman's cap. On the deck, I clung to the frame of the hatch and watched in awe as the ship's bow submerged forty feet. With fearsome power it lurched up and washed the deck with huge waves. The propeller at the stern of the ship took its turn and lifted above the water, crashing back down into the waves.

Suddenly, a gust of wind grabbed my hat. Instinctively, I reached out for it and let go of the doorway. My body sailed like a rag after the hat and slammed against a rope that was stretched along the edge of the boat. I clung to it and, hand over hand, made my way to the stairway. I did not go for any more fresh breaths of air.

Almost a month after we had left Great Britain, in the winter of 1940, we arrived at the dock in Halifax, Canada, glad to be airmen!

We traveled by train across vast expanses of Canadian grandeur. Beautiful, but cold. The cold cut through us like a knife. The citizens of Winnipeg, alerted that British soldiers were to arrive at the train depot at a certain time, came by the hundreds to get their first glimpse of soldiers from the front lines. Our officers gave us two hours to fraternize with them.

A pretty young girl came up to me and introduced herself. "My name is Nancy. How was your trip?" she asked.

"Long!" I admitted, then changed the subject. "Your weather is cold here, but your welcome sure is warm! Thank you for coming out to see us."

"My mother said that I could invite someone home to a meal. Here is our address for when you have time off." She extended a little hand-printed card to me.

Just then another girl came up to me. I quickly stuffed the card into my pocket, and shortly, there was another address to join it. The two hours flew by, and we were ordered onto trucks.

The Canadian barracks were long, low buildings that accommodated sixty men. A big pot-bellied stove kept us from the unbelievably penetrating cold. The temperature often dropped below zero. Also, snow drifted and piled against the buildings, hangars, and across the airfield. Sometimes we awoke in the morning to six feet of snow heaped against the door.

Every two weeks, we were given two days off. To get away from the barracks, I called Nancy, the first girl that had come up to me at the train depot, and was invited to a meal at her home. The hospitality and food were wonderful. I was introduced to foods I'd never seen before: roast turkey, corn on the cob, and scrumptious strawberry shortcake with ice cream. After the meal, I was taken to another new experience, a hockey game. I marveled at the speed and dexterity of the men as they skimmed across the ice on skates, slashing with their sticks at the puck in front of them.

Our new life in Canada was relaxed compared to bomb alerts and air raids in England. I started a jazz band that consisted of an accordion, a saxophone, my trumpet, and drums. We played for dances and other social occasions. When men were sent home to England, we went to the station and played a farewell to them. When new troops arrived, we met them in the same hospitable fashion.

On one trip to a social evening, an acquaintance asked me, "Ware, what's your first name?"

"Edward."

"Is that what your family calls you?"

"No, they use Eddie, but I don't like it. Sounds a bit feminine to me."

"I know what you mean. My name is Robert, and I don't mind being called Bob, but Bobby reminds me of socks!" We both laughed. Then he asked, "What about 'Ted,' that's a nickname for Edward."

"Yes! That's better than Eddie and less formal than Edward. I'll use it!"

"By the way, Ted, do you have a steady girl back home?"

"No, I don't. Why?"

"Oh, I just noticed that you don't write much, and you don't get a lot of mail." Just then the train stopped for us to get off.

Time went fast in Canada, especially through the sum-mer and gorgeous colors of fall. During the second winter, I contracted pneumonia and was sent to the hospital for a few weeks. The Daughters of the British Empire came to the hospital, gave us cookies, and invited us to their homes.

One family that befriended me was the Shuefelts. They were ten years older than I, with a baby daughter named Beverly. I spent many hours in their delightful company. At the end of a year, I received extended leave of about ten days and took a trip with the Shuefelts to America, where I saw Yellowstone Park.

The following year, I took a train trip to New York City with another friend. We wore our uniform and visited servicemen's clubs. Americans went out of their way to en-tertain us. We were taken to a Broadway show and watched women swoon over Frank Sinatra. I had never seen any-thing like it! We sat in the back of the large auditorium and watched as various entertainers came on stage. The crowd was rude and unruly and booed everyone but Sinatra. One entertainer played a banjo. Someone threw a coin on the stage at him, which is the height of entertainment insults. The player stopped his performance, looked down at the audience with absolute disdain, and said, "Who threw that coin?" The hall became quiet. He finished his act.

Sinatra came on next, and the crowd started to coo and scream. Some women fainted while he sang. My friend turned to me. "Can you believe it?"

"No, I can't understand it!"

We visited bars and clubs where jazz music was played. We met Louis Armstrong, Lionel Hampton, Gene Krupa, and Bud Freeman. Of course, we went to see New York City's famous lady, the Statue of Liberty.

On our way back to Canada, we stopped at Niagara Falls, and were awed by the powerful falls and their rugged beauty. Afterward, we returned to the depot to board the next train to Canada. It was full, so we split up looking for empty seats. My buddy took the first empty seat he could find. I looked around and saw a seat beside a young woman. As I sat down beside her she shouted, "Look at this man! Pig! He's trying to get fresh with me!"

Baffled, I looked around to see whom she referred to and realized that she meant me! "No, madam! This is the only seat available! I have no such intentions!"

"All men are alike. I hate you all. You're all pigs!" She said loudly.

"I'm sorry to hear you say that. You probably have had reason to think so." I was furtively looking for somewhere to escape.

"My husband was killed in France. Why should he have been sent over there anyway? I hate him for going and leaving me."

It was the first time I viewed the war from the perspective of a woman. I was relieved that I did not have a wife to hate me for a choice that was made for me. She continued to berate all males. Before another seat became available, she had run out of verbal ammunition and started to get friendly, even brazen. I was delighted when she got out at the next train station.

As I thought of my home in England, I sometimes felt guilty that my life in Canada was so good and my loved ones were suffering privations. My mother wrote to me every week. I received two or three letters from my father while I was overseas.

I was enjoying Canada. I had a couple of girlfriends whom I went to dances with, but I wasn't really interested in them. One by one my buddies, most of them younger than I, married Canadian girls.

I decided it was time for me to make some important decisions regarding my future. On a beautiful fall afternoon, I went for a walk and sat down on the grass, leaned up against a tall pine tree, and I began to think of all of the girls I knew. Whom would I want to spend the rest of my life with? There was Nancy, a nice Canadian girl. . . . If I married her I could stay in Canada. For some reason the thought did not keep my attention. Then there was Lily, a pretty girl with rich parents who had been quite friendly. My heart did not stir at that suggestion either.

I thought of British girls, Jean from Bow, and Nelly, the friendly nurse. Fun memories, but that was all. I lay back on the green earth and looked up at the blue sky. My heart beat faster. What was it about that beautiful blue? I closed my eyes and saw the same blue in a certain little country lassie's eyes. Milly Halliday, of course! I sat bolt upright, my thoughts fully alert. Where could she be? Maybe she was married, or had died in a bomb, or wanted nothing to do with me! After all, I hadn't seen her in ten years. I no longer was content to stay in Canada. I became restless and counted the days until I would be sent back to England. Maybe, just maybe, Milly wasn't married. . . .

I was repatriated to England in February of 1944. I decided to go to see Mrs. Halliday, Milly's mother, as soon as possible. I must find out where Milly was. After the ship docked, I was transported to my new assignment, an airfield seventy miles from London. I then bought a motorcycle and traveled home to my family and, hopefully, to Milly.

The pall of smoke from burnt buildings was visible miles before I reached London's outskirts. The streets were clogged with rubble. I had to get off of my cycle and push it. I passed weary, stumbling firemen, almost asleep on their feet, methodically hosing out the fires. Bandaged, dazed homeowners shuffled along as they sifted through their home's charred remains. A lump rose in my throat that nearly choked me, what if my street was in tatters?

To my great relief, I found my parents' home and neighborhood undamaged. They were delighted to see me and kept me busy recounting my experiences. My brother Cliff had grown taller than I, yet was still the jovial young man I remembered. My sister was more beautiful than ever. She had many American suitors, but was most interested in a British sailor, Ron Giles.

Finally, I mustered the courage and found the opportunity to visit the Halliday home. I was facing my worst fear: Milly would be married. Timidly, I knocked at the front entrance. Mrs. Halliday opened the door. "Edward Ware! I am so glad to see you! Oh, this is wonderful! Do come in." She made me feel so welcome. "Come in and have a cup of tea!"

After I sat down, I asked her about the war and how it had affected her family. As politely and diplomatically as I knew, I went through names of the family. "How is your husband and John? And how about Ruth and Gladys, Elsie and Grace?" And, casually, I asked, "Now, Milly. She's married, of course?"

"No! No!" Mrs. Halliday said.

"Oh! Oh! Well, that's nice." My heart was pounding.

"She's due home any minute."

Just then the front door opened and a sweet voice called, "Hello Mummy! I'm home!"

When Milly entered the dining room, I knew I could not live without her. She was the same sweet-faced, blue-eyed English country girl I had remembered.

After her initial look of surprise, she seemed indifferent to me. Planning cautiously, I didn't ask her to go out, but I left determined to marry her. I thought and thought about a strategy to achieve my goal.

After I returned to my base, I tried to write to her. I crumpled up every letter. None of them seemed good enough. However, after many crumpled letters, I decided it was better to send an imperfect letter and give her the opportunity to make a decision about me than to wait until I could come up with a perfect letter that might be too late. I sealed my heart with the letter and mailed it. Days went by. Finally, I received my answer that gave me hope.

As soon as I was given time off, I went to see Milly at the hospital, where she stayed. We discussed our past experiences and our hopes and plans for the future. After a few months courtship, I asked her to marry me. To my ecstatic joy, she agreed!

I braved the bombs of London as often as I could get leave to see her. I also saved all of my cigarettes to trade for chocolate, which I carefully wrapped and sent to her. It was a delight to please her.

During one of my visits, Milly told me that Reverend Rose, her pastor, wanted to see me. With some anxiety, I made an appointment with the vicar. After I was seated in his office, I confidently answered his first question: "Edward, do you love Milly?"

"Yes sir, I do, with all of my heart."

"I assume that Milly has told you that she might not be able to have children? How do you feel about that?" he asked.

"Well, sir, I feel that my life has no meaning without Milly. Children would be nice, but it is she that I cannot live without."

"And, Edward," he continued, "Milly is a Christian girl and must not marry an unbeliever."

"Reverend Rose, I know that I am not all that I should be, but I have certainly accepted Christ as my Savior, and I do desire to please Him and have Him work in my life."

"That is all that can be asked. You'll find, Edward, that the more you love the Lord Jesus, the more your earthly relationships will flourish. Milly is a loving, giving, wonderful girl. If you will love her as yourself, she will give you a wonderful life." He appeared satisfied with our interview, which pleased Milly immensely.

Later, we rode to town and chose her engagement ring. Her hand trembled as I placed it on her finger. Three diamonds on her ring represented three words: "I love you."

Reverend Rose and members of his congregation gave us our wedding and then surprised us with a beautiful honeymoon. However, no scenery, no honeymoon, or wonderful accommodations could compare with the delight of being married to Milly. She was all that I had dreamed of and more.

After our honeymoon, Milly returned to the hospital, and I, to my air base. I took every opportunity to see her. She was a senior and was able to switch duty times with other nurses when I could get leave.

Sometimes we went to my parents' home where they tried to give us privacy.

One evening, before my parents left for a night out, they suggested, "Pretend the house is yours. Cook what you wish for your supper."

After they left, I sat down to read a book as Milly worked excitedly in the kitchen. When she was ready, she called me to the table, where I was surprised with a beautiful plate of food served with the best china and silverware.

"Milly, these greens are delicious!" I praised her cooking, as I remembered the hated greens of my youth. "How did you make them so fresh tasting?"

"My mum taught me," she said, and then looked a little sad. Milly's mother had died five months before we were married.

"She would have been happy to see us now, wouldn't she?" I added, also saddened that the lovely lady had not lived longer.

"I wish she could hear what I have to tell you." Milly had a twinkle in her eye.

"What's that, dear?"

"You're going to be a father."

"A what?"

"A father. I wasn't sure about it, but now I am!" Milly's eyes shone.

I jumped up, and we danced around the room in each other's arms.

We danced again on VE (Victory in Europe) Day and rejoiced also when the war in the Pacific was over (VJ Day). With no more air raids, weeks went by at the base without official orders.

Having completed seven years in the air force, I was anxious to get back to civilian life to earn more money for my wife and expected child.

On September 3, 1945, I was called from a plane to the main office. "You're a father, Ware! You may take three days off!"

I had just sold my motorcycle and bought an old Singer car. It was a wreck. The steering wheel wiggled so much that I had almost to come to a full stop to keep it from wobbling. Somehow I managed to drive to the hospital where I found Milly, radiant, in bed. I ran to her. I felt overwhelmed with love for her. After a few moments, I realized she had something to share with me. I looked into her blue eyes and then to where she pointed. It was a bassinet in the corner of the room.

"Our baby!"

"Yes, our baby, Kevin." It was the name we had agreed upon. I walked over to meet my firstborn son.

A few months later, the flight school closed, and we were all demobilized from military service. I drove to Cambridge, where the government had a big deployment center. I exchanged my uniforms and equipment for a new civilian suit, shirt, and tie. My severance pay wasn't much, but it was enough to give us a little money to begin our lives together.

I drove back to where Milly was living with her sister Ruth, and from there we began our civilian lives.

To earn money, I started another dance band while I was seeking a new job. Milly was not enthusiastic about the band but agreed with my motives. She always went with me to the dances, but didn't dance. Instead, she sat on the sidelines and enjoyed talking with others who were watching the dancers. Milly became pregnant again, and as the baby developed, she felt uncomfortable at the dances.

"Would you mind if I stayed home?" she asked me one night.

"No, darling, of course not. I'll move the evening along quickly and rush home."

One night at the dance, a young girl made all sorts of unwanted suggestions. "You sure are a handsome fellow. Would you like to come home with me?"

"Excuse me, miss, but I'm married," I told her, and thought that would end the matter. When we closed that night, to my horror, she was waiting for me outside.

She grabbed my arm, "Come with me. We can have a good time together."

I broke away from her and ran home. When I entered the house, I threw my trumpet onto the bed and said, "I've had enough. I don't want any more of that!" So ended my dance band career.

A few days later in Coulsdon, I saw an unusual van drive up to a garage. The side windows of the van showed many tools inside. Intrigued, I realized I was looking at a traveling tool store. I told the driver that I would be interested in a job.

"I have worked with tools, all kinds of tools, all of my life, and I've also been a salesman."

He was interested in me and took my address. A few days later, I was invited for an interview with the company's manager, and I got the job!

Full of enthusiasm and determination to do well, I drove the van to garages, machine shops, and engineering works. Because there was such a shortage of tools after the war, I found people eager to buy. I sold by commission and soon earned an excellent salary.

As time passed, I sensed that the owners were unhappy with their decision to pay me a commission. I was now bringing home more than they thought a salesman should make.

On October 26, 1946, our second son, Clive, arrived. We were a happy, blessed family.

One day, as we took a ride in a new vehicle that I had just purchased, out of the blue, I asked Milly, "Would you consider moving to Canada with me?"

I could tell that she was surprised, but she did not miss a beat. She responded, "Eddie, like Ruth in the Bible, I say, 'where you go, I will go.' You've been to Canada and know what it is like. If you think it is a good idea for us to move there, I will back you up."

Joy surged through me. "You're a wonderful wife, Milly. I'm so grateful that you married me!"

A Nurse Makes Big Choices, 1944–1946

I was humming as I got off the bus at my parent's stop. Things were going well for me. I enjoyed nursing and looked forward to an exciting career as a registered nurse. I had a few hours off to visit my parents. The sky was blue and clear of enemy planes. My mind jumped from one happy thought to another as I entered the Halliday gate.

I found Mother in the living room with a guest.

I gulped. To my utter surprise, there stood Edward Ware.

"Milly! So glad to see you! I just got back from Canada."

It was hard to bridge ten years in two minutes. The last I had heard of him he had a girl friend.

I felt shy as I faced this handsome man. "Nice to see you, Eddie."

"Will you be home for long?" he asked.

"No, only an hour or two. I have to be back on duty this evening."

"I must leave right away, since I promised Mother that I would only be gone a minute. She was pulling lunch out of the oven when I left. I hope you won't mind seeing me again?"

"That would be fine."

He beamed and excused himself.

As mother closed the front door, she said, "He sure is a nice boy, isn't he, Milly?"

"He's all right," I said casually, contradicting the flutter of my heart.

In the weeks that followed, I tried hard to think only of my upcoming final exams. However, a letter I received from Eddie, addressed from an air base in the north of England, interrupted my commitment.

"My Dear Milly," Eddie's letter began, "This, I think, is going to be full of surprises for you. Three times I have tried to write but didn't know how to start. What I have in mind has been slowly resolving in me, born of months of thought and worry that I might be too late.

"Milly, I must tell you that I am very, very much in love with you. Very humbly I ask, 'Will you have me?' Because if you want me I am yours, only and always. . . . Please write me and tell me 'yes' or 'no'. . . . I haven't much to offer you, but everything I did or will do, would be for you. . . . It would make me so happy if you said 'yes'. . . ."

My heart spun as I danced around in my room with the letter in my hand. Then I stopped and thought, *Why should his letter send me into ecstasies? We have not communicated in years.* I put the letter in my pocket and carried it with me on the ward. *How should I write back?* I must finish nursing before I could make a commitment, yet I didn't want to ignore his proposal. *What should I say?*

A few nights later, there was a terrifying air raid. The matron shouted, "In between checks of the patients, sit in the linen closet, and if a bomb hits the hospital, you'll hopefully come out with the living."

I could hear the bombs striking closer, so close that I was convinced the next one would land on the hospital. As

I faced imminent death, I knew I didn't want to die without telling Eddie that I was interested in him. I found a writing pad and wrote from the closet:

Dear Eddie,

You were quite right when you said your letter was full of surprises! How I wish you were here beside me to talk things over. Perhaps not at this time, or "here," since I am on the tuberculosis ward tonight, in charge of fifty patients and three nurses. I'm getting a lot of interruptions!. . . It has been years since we knew each other well, and I know that I have changed (whether for better or worse, I leave you to decide). I believe that you have also. With this in mind, I would like to know you better. I am quite prepared to give you the chance to prove to me that you mean what you say. Nursing at the moment takes up most of my time. I finish my training in April and then take the state final to become an RN in September. I have made no set plans after that. I wouldn't bother to answer your letter if I weren't interested in you. Perhaps after we have met and talked things over, I shall realize it is not a dream and be less reserved. . . .

Yours sincerely,
Milly

I posted my letter and waited. In my off-duty hours, I sorted my feelings: a heart that raced at the very thought of him; a contented peace at the sound of the name, Mrs. Edward Ware. However, I worried that when I told him I could not have children, he would lose interest in me. I even fretted that my aloofness would turn him off. As I considered the total picture, I came to the conclusion that I really loved

Eddie, and if in truth he loved me, any other person or plans would be insignificant.

As I was making this life changing decision, my mother was unexpectedly admitted to our hospital. She was seriously ill. The doctor recommended a complete hysterectomy. However, she was so ill that surgery was postponed for a week. As much as I had become interested in communicating with Eddie and planning our future together, I gave my mother first priority. Her critical condition, as well as my other responsibilities, took precedence. My plans and emotions were placed on hold.

Following her surgery, mother continued to have complications. During this physically exhausting time, I was given two nights off duty and was encouraged to get some rest. Assured by all the staff that they would tenderly care for Mother, I took the bus to Doctor Lenanten's house to sleep.

In the middle of the night, the phone rang. "Sorry to have to call you, Nurse, but your mother has taken a turn for the worse. We think you should come."

Doctor Lenanton was also awake and insisted that she accompany me. We drove to my father's house to pick him up and rushed to the hospital.

"Oh, I should have been there," I wailed as we drove along. "Maybe I could have done something!"

As soon as we arrived at the ward, I was given her report: "Mrs. Halliday's abdomen is distended, and her fever is 105 degrees Fahrenheit. She is in a coma."

We dashed to her room. The doctors backed away and allowed us to touch her. She breathed a few more breaths, and then she was gone.

Doctor Lenanton put her arms around me as I stood, stunned.

I watched my father drop to his knees. He raised his hands and prayed, "Father, I give you back my wonderful wife."

I watched in horror. Daddy doesn't love Mother! How could he take her death so peacefully! Surely he did not care for her!

The matron came over and kissed me on the cheek. "Are you going home with your father?"

"No. I am going back to work." I announced, and left the room.

I was furious and was also in an abyss of anguish and grief. My mother was gone; my father didn't care; and where was God?

As I entered the ward, I couldn't remember which ward it was, nor what I should be doing for the sleeping patients. In shock, I wandered dazed onto a dark, empty verandah that overlooked a lake. Standing silently for a few moments to regain my composure, I instinctively raised my hands and cried out, "God, I've lost my mother! I can't lose you, too! I give you back my mother. I thank you for her." Suddenly my despair was gone. I was filled with peace and joy.

I was now ready to return to my parents' home with my father.

The house was soon filled with flowers. As was the custom, Mummy's body lay in the sitting room for a week as friends and family came to mourn.

Reverend Vine, who had married my parents many years before in the Baptist church in Wrotham, spoke at her funeral. He eulogized her life, noting how she loved and cared for her family. "She has not gone; she has just gone ahead," he reminded us.

A few months later, in our hospital, my mother's sister, Aunt Ada, died as I held her in my arms. She fought cancer and lost.

To compound my sorrow, a distant relative of Aunt Ada, who had never been close to her, nor visited her in the hospital, insisted that all Aunt Ada's worldly goods should go to him. Uncle Harold, Aunt Ada's brother, asked me, "Don't you want to get anything of Aunt Ada's?"

"No," I said sadly. "I've got memories. That's all I need. It makes me feel bad that Aunt Ada's loving memory should be tainted by selfishness." He nodded.

Following a rainstorm, a rainbow often appears, contrasting the hours of gloomy gray. After my shattering grief, I glimpsed my rainbow. Another letter from Eddie arrived! He asked to see me. He also set a time and place, and my heart flooded with hope and anticipation.

Eddie and I met at the appointed time and talked about our past, present, and future. I told him about the doctor's concerns that I would not be able to have a baby. "Milly, dear, it's you that I can't live without. Whether we have children or not, it's all right."

Discarding my indifference, I told him that I cared for him and would be happy to be his wife. His response was electrifying. He sent me on a trip into the skies to join my rainbow as he gave me my first kiss.

My life changed. I no longer worried over exams and earning good grades. I had chosen to marry Eddie.

I felt the enchantment of his love as he risked fires, air raids, and much danger to come see me. He bartered his ration coupons to be able to surprise me with chocolates.

As often as we were able, we visited each other's families. During one visit to my father's house, there was an air raid.

Daddy shouted, "Everybody to the air raid shelter! Nobody's allowed to sleep in the house tonight."

Eddie and I would have preferred to stay in the house and talk all night. To our dismay, we had no alternative but to obey.

My father ushered me to the bunk above my sister Grace. Eddie was sent to the bunk below my other sister. I was annoyed that he did not trust us to be together, nor was he sensitive to our desire to be alone.

Despite these interruptions and inconveniences, we set our wedding date for October 21, 1944. My government RN exams came first, so I was relieved when Reverend Rose called me. "We, your friends, are going to give you your wedding and honeymoon. You don't have to worry about a thing. You just show up and everything will be ready."

I was to show up with everything ready, except I did not have a wedding dress. I took time from studying for my exams to pray for one! I had no clothing ration coupons, so could not go out and purchase one.

Movie studios in Hollywood, California, had sent boxes of wedding dresses to our college of nursing with the note, "These are for nurses who are getting married and can't afford wedding dresses."

Hoping I would find one that would fit, I tried many of them on. However, I was disappointed. I was uncomfortable in the beautiful but skimpy wedding dresses.

One of Eddie's aunts rescued me. She offered her wedding dress. "I have a wedding dress all tucked away that you may use." It fit me perfectly, and I felt comfortably modest in it.

After my dress was chosen, I selected my attendants. I invited an old friend, Alice Ingram, from my childhood days in Kent, and Eddie's sister, Joan, to be my bridesmaids. With these decisions behind me, I went back to studying.

Exam day arrived. As I completed the last question and handed the test in, I breathed a sigh of relief. I did not worry about the results, since I had my wedding to think of! Two weeks later, I received notification that I had passed. My

Christian friends and I celebrated quietly. War did not allow for costly parties.

War influenced many things. The day before the wedding, Alice called. "Milly, I can't come. They won't let me off work. I'm sorry."

"That's okay, Alice. You can't help it that we're in a war. We'll miss you." It was one thing for a bridesmaid to not show up, but I trembled to think of what would be far worse.

"What if Eddie isn't allowed the time off? What will we do?" I asked Mrs. Mason.

"Milly, 'be anxious for nothing, but in everything by prayer and supplication let your requests be made known unto God.' It seems funny for me to be telling you Scripture verses, but I'm sure it will all work out as we've all been praying." Just as Mrs. Mason assured, Eddie arrived at his parents' home just after midnight on the day of the wedding.

Since I was not allowed to see Eddie until the wedding, I sent him a note with my brother John: "I'm so glad you made it. Just a few more hours! Love you. Milly"

He responded: "All of the generals in the world could not have prevented me! We will soon be united forever. I love you. Your Eddie"

In the morning, I enjoyed the excitement of having my hair styled. My father went with me to pick up my floral bouquet. When he saw that I had chosen red roses, he reminded me, "No, dear, pink is your color." We were able to exchange the red roses for a beautiful pink rose floral arrangement.

Following these preparations, a taxi took us to meet Reverend Rose. As we arrived in the vestibule, I could see that the sanctuary was full, and the choir had lined the aisle. I glanced at the front of the church and saw Eddie was there waiting for me. His brother was standing beside him. I smiled at my father and gave his arm a squeeze. The choir started to sing. As the organist played the wedding march I walked down the aisle on my father's arm.

Eddie's face was radiant as his eyes met mine. I was certain of his love and devotion.

Back row: Joseph Ware, Clifford Ware,
Edward Ware, me, Joan Ware, John Halliday
Front Row: Florence Ware,
David Mash (my nephew), Mrs. Mason

The service proceeded solemnly; I promised to "love, honor, and obey," as Eddie repeated earnestly, "With my body, I thee worship." After we had repeated our vows and were pronounced man and wife, the choir formed an honor guard and sang a recessional as we joyously arm-in-arm walked down the aisle. It began to rain, so we stayed in the vestibule and greeted our guests.

We spent our first night together in a lovely room at a golf course clubhouse, provided by my church friends. The following morning, Reverend Rose served us communion. We also reverently placed my rose bridal bouquet on Mother's grave. From the cemetery, we were taken to the train station in London. As we waved goodbye to all our friends, they cheered and clapped. We were so blessed by the many demonstrations of their love.

The train was full of exhausted British soldiers. They lay on the floor, the luggage racks, and on us. We were relieved when we arrived at the privacy of our honeymoon farmhouse, despite the primitive bathroom facilities of a ceramic pot, stored conveniently under our bed.

During the day we walked along the gorgeous coastal cliffs of Tintagel and shared with each other our dreams and hopes for the future.

"What shall we do after the war, Milly?"

"Whatever you think. My happiness is being with you."

Our honeymoon ended too soon. As in every flight, we had soared to heights of love and sharing, and now had to touch down to the reality of our daily routine.

England was still at war and required that we do our part. Eddie returned to his air force base, and I, to the hospital. I returned reenergized and totally in love.

We wrote to each other and planned our schedule to see each other once a month. Whenever I got news that my husband had leave, the nursing staff kindly filled in for me, so that I could spend time with him. Usually, we met at his parents' home, since they were romantically inclined, understood our need to be alone, and were always very thoughtful of us.

One evening after supper, Mother Ware told us, "Milly, for ten long years your sweet mother and I agreed and prayed that God would keep you and Eddie for each other, and look! God heard and answered our prayers!"

A few months after we were married, God answered my most fervent prayer. Contrary to my doctor's warning that I would not have children, I became pregnant. I stayed at the hospital on duty until the end of my seventh month then took a leave of absence and traveled north to be near Eddie. I lived with a dear old woman who insisted that I was in a "holy state" and wasn't to do anything, not even walk up stairs. I didn't dare tell her of all the stairs that I had climbed and the work I had done in the hospital during the seven months of my "holy state."

Unexpectedly, Eddie was transferred to a base farther south. We decided I should move temporarily to my father's home. Shortly after that, I moved in with my sister Ruth and her family.

When our firstborn arrived on September 3, 1945, Eddie could not be with me. We had already decided on the baby's name, Kevin Edward.

"What a wonderful, beautiful child you are!" I cooed to him. "I can't wait for you to meet your daddy!" Shortly after, my handsome husband arrived.

"Sweetheart, what a beautiful, tremendous woman you are!" He greeted me with a big kiss. His words made me feel warm, and his kiss thrilled me. I pointed to the bassinet, and he tiptoed over to meet our little man. Eddie's face was aglow as he examined the baby's precious little hands and feet. "We sure have a lot to be thankful for, don't we, Milly?"

Baby Kevin met many people in those first days: my nursing friends, Grandfather and Grandmother Ware, Grandfather Halliday, and all of the uncles and aunts.

Reverend Rose also came and gave a prayer of dedication for Kevin. Then to my complete surprise, he generously offered us his home. "My wife and I are taking a month leave from the parish. We would like you, Eddie, and Baby Kevin to stay in the rectory while we are gone." A few days later, I was released from the hospital to spend a glorious month in the parish with my new family.

Before the month had passed for Reverend Rose and his wife to return home, we searched everywhere for a place to rent. There were absolutely no vacancies. Our best choice was to move in with my father again.

Kevin and his Grandfather Halliday became very close. My father was an early riser, so he lifted Kevin from his crib when Kevin first woke up, and thoughtfully took him to the rose garden, where they spent many happy hours. We were able to continue our sleep.

When Kevin started to toddle around the house and garden, his grandfather taught him many things. When he got too close to the rose bushes, my father pressed his little finger against a sharp thorn. Kevin cried but stayed away from the thorny bushes.

The next year, on October 26, Kevin had a little brother! How we again rejoiced for all our blessings when Clive Philip arrived! Our only frustration was not having our own home. Of course, my father was kind and generous, but we needed more living space.

One day Eddie asked, "Milly, would you be willing to go to the New World with me?"

Needless to say, within a few weeks following my positive answer, we were at the London airport, ready to embark for Canada.

To Canada as a Family, 1946–1947

I will follow where you lead," Milly had said as we walked along the cliffs of Tintagel on our honeymoon. At the time, they were romantic words, and I loved her for them, but when she put those words into action, my imaginative spirit was freed. I felt like a whole man, able to do anything.

Milly's trust made me take our future very seriously. After much thought, and considering all our alternatives, the best opportunities I saw for us were in the New World. Of course, I was thrilled when Milly supported my decision to move.

I researched methods of transportation to Canada. Ships were booked months in advance. A few airplanes were available but completely booked.

One day, I was talking with a friend about the shortage of housing in England versus the building opportunities in Canada. "I've been considering moving to Canada, but transportation from here is as impossible to find as housing."

He suggested, "There's a small new airline called El Al that flies to Canada and Israel. Maybe they'd have something."

I found the phone number and called them a few days later. A courteous agent responded to my request. "We fly to Canada once a week. The flights are completely booked right now, but if you wish to leave your name and number, we will put you on our waiting list. If we get a cancellation, we'll call you." I left our name and number but did not expect to hear from them.

However, the next week the telephone did ring. It was El Al. "Mr. Ware, if you and your family can be ready in two days, we can fly you to Canada."

I couldn't believe it. "Okay. We'll take it. I will be by your office tomorrow to purchase the tickets."

"Purchase what, Dear?" Milly asked as she entered the hallway to the bedroom. Her arms were full of fresh laundry from the clothesline.

Dazed, I responded, "Our flight to Canada." She nearly dropped the stack of laundered diapers.

"When? How?" Her pretty face was slightly pale.

"In two days. Can we do it?"

We both sat on the edge of the bed and looked at each other. We hugged for a good, long while. Then she pushed me back, and with her beautiful, kind, blue eyes slightly misty said, "Yes, Dear, we can do it. But we've got to get to work immediately!"

I hugged her again until she squealed and then began our whirlwind preparation for our trip to Canada. We made a list of what we had to do and whom we had to call. We gave things away, sold our car and what little furniture we owned, and miraculously arrived at the London Airport in two days with our children and quota of boxes.

The El Al Constellation took off with us belted in our seats, heading north, and then west. We stopped en route both in Scotland and in Iceland for fuel. We were fed six eggs during one evening meal, and we savored every delicious mouthful.

When we landed in Montreal, Canada, we were exhausted but excited. A friend in England had given me the name of his daughter who lived there. When we contacted her and told her we came with gifts from her father, she welcomed us warmly into her big home.

That first night after everyone had gone to bed, Clive woke up hungry and started to cry. His tummy was still on British time. We were not prepared for him to awaken hungry during the night. "Eddie, he needs a glass of warm milk. What shall we do?" Milly whispered as she rocked Clive back and forth to soothe him.

"I don't know, but we can't wake up the household. Get him dressed, and I'll go out and see what I can find." I pulled on some clothes and walked with him outside. With Clive in my arms, I searched for an open store or restaurant. Thankfully, I saw a trucker's diner with the lights on. As I entered the diner, the lady behind the counter looked up at me, and Clive started to cry again. She gave me a nasty look, deciding I was either a delinquent parent or a kidnapper.

"May I bother you for a glass of milk?"

"Shouldn't the baby be in bed?" she asked as she poured a glass of milk. As soon as I raised it to Clive's lips, he stopped his crying and began to slurp hungrily.

"I know this looks peculiar, but we just flew in from England, and the baby is still on a British time schedule."

"Oh, you poor dears. I'm so sorry. Is there anything I can do for you?" She refused to let me pay for the milk and packed some cookies in a bag for a snack later.

Our new adventure in Canada continued the next day as we took a train to Milly's Aunt Ruth in Chatham, Ontario. On the way, Kevin complained, "My tummy hurts." Before

Milly or I could respond, Kevin started to fill his pants. He had been trained for over a year, so we had not anticipated any accidents. His little English suit was soiled, and he started to cry. I took him to the train toilet where I found it quite a job to clean him up. "I'm sorry, Daddy, I couldn't help it," he said.

"Of course, you couldn't. You've been a big boy. The food and time zones are different here; that's why it happened."

That I was no longer a bachelor, but responsible for the well being of my children and family became a reality.

After I settled Kevin back in his seat, Milly mentioned that she did not feel well.

"Darling," I replied, "you worked so hard before we left, and now the time zones are different. It's understandable." I kept my eye on her, though, and noticed as we traveled that her face was drawn and dark circles formed under her eyes.

At last we arrived at Aunt Ruth's home and were warmly welcomed. The kind woman, happy to see her relatives again, played with the boys, waited on us, and fed us delicious meals.

I immediately looked for work. Even though I had brought some tools with me, no one needed anything fixed or built. I tried to sell my salesman abilities but found no sales opportunities.

A few days later, a fair came to town and advertised for workers. I signed up. It was heavy labor. Huge pieces of steel had to be connected to set up a ferris wheel. From dawn to dusk, I toiled for thirty-five cents an hour. The boss was very demanding and gruff. At the end of the job, when we went for our wages, we found that we were each shorted several dollars. Outraged, I complained. I was then told that they were out of cash, and we should be glad for any. Some of my fellow worker's plight was more serious than mine, and I was angry and frustrated.

Following this injustice, I answered an ad for a carpentry job and was hired. I learned to lay bowling alley floors. I was instructed to nail one-inch-by-four inch wide strips of hard maple wood together to a height of four feet. These boards were then turned on their side and became a section of the bowling alley floor. During the first hour on the job, I broke the handle of my hammer, so I hurried to a nearby hardware store and bought another. At the time, I was unaware that hammers came in different weights. The hammer I bought was the least expensive and quite light. I later realized that the lightweight tool took more energy and time to drive the long, coated nails into the rock-hard wood.

When I returned to work I only finished a third of the height required. The foreman came, looked at what I had finished, and sent me to start a new section while he completed that one. Back on my knees, I struggled to nail the next section. When the boards were a height comfortable to work on, the foreman returned to finish the easy nailing. He sent me to begin another section. By this time my hands, unused to this manual labor, were blistered and bloody. Disregarding the pain, I continued my hammering. I had a wife and family to support. The wages were eighty cents an hour, which was good pay.

After a week of doing my best, the foreman came to me. "I'm going to have to lay you off. You're not fast enough." I was devastated.

To compound my worries, back at Aunt Ruth's house, Milly was experiencing terrible pain. Since she also had a fever, we took her to a doctor.

After she was examined, the physician stated somberly, "Your wife has a severe kidney infection. Her kidneys are deteriorating, and if the fever increases, she should be hospitalized. The excess protein in her body, after years of restriction, has caused it."

When we drove back to Aunt Ruth's, the boys met us at the door. "Aunty Ruth said that the doctors were going to make Mummy better!"

Milly was pale and trembling as I tucked her under the covers. She gave the boys a wan smile and closed her eyes.

"Why isn't she better?" Kevin whispered. Just then Aunt Ruth stepped in and took the boys to dinner.

"Come and eat, Eddie," Aunt Ruth suggested.

"I can't eat." Food would have choked me; the lump was so large in my throat.

I grabbed my hat and went out the back door of the house, tears coursing down my cheeks.

A few blocks away, I spotted an empty park bench. I sat down and put my head in my cracked, bruised hands. I agonized, "What have I done? What shall I do? What can I do? Please God, show me what I must do. Shall I take her back to England and call off this venture?"

From my inner depths came a strong impression, "No, don't go home. Go on." Peace and assurance flooded my mind. Even though Milly was too ill to travel, I felt sure that God had given guidance, and somehow we were to follow it. Suddenly, I had to speak with Milly.

I hurried back to the house and entered the back door. In our room, I got on my knees by my sweetheart's bed, touched her pillow, and gently wiped her damp forehead. "Darling, I think I know what we're supposed to do."

"What's that, Eddie?" she whispered.

"Leave Chatham and go on to Vancouver."

"As we discussed on the plane coming over?" Her blood-shot eyes looked deeply into mine. "We don't have the money for a car yet."

"That's my problem, Milly."

Since she was a nurse, she knew that she was very ill and should be going to a hospital, not Vancouver. And yet, she said, "If that's what you think we should do, Eddie, let's go."

Within two days, an unexpected advance of eight hundred dollars from our savings in England arrived, and I was able to buy an old 1938 six-cylinder Chevrolet from a traveling salesman that I happened to meet. It had high mileage, but the engine ran well.

That evening Aunt Ruth took me aside. "Young man, I am Milly's only relative here, and I feel like her mother. If you take her away from the help she needs, you will kill her. She is too ill to care for the boys, and I am warning you, you are embarking on a foolish, senseless errand. Do not go!"

I listened and then went to Milly's bedside. "Darling, what do you want me to do? If you think that we should stay, we will."

"Eddie, I trust your direction. Let's go," she replied. Her faith in me and my connection to God, humbled me as nothing had ever done. I packed our belongings and prepared the boys for the trip.

On July 4, 1947, after prayer in our room for God's mercy, guidance, and healing, we got into the car and waved goodbye to Aunt Ruth.

Since I had heard that roads were faster and gas was cheaper in America, we headed south. My strategy was to travel through the northern part of the United States and into Washington, then turn back into Canada.

During the first and second day of our journey, I witnessed a divine miracle: to my amazement, color returned to Milly's cheeks, her fever disappeared, and the sparkle in her lovely eyes came back. She became actively involved in my plans for the trip.

"I'm feeling better!" she announced with a lilt in her voice. From that moment, she was perfectly well! We could only explain the miracle as God's message of approval.

To reach America, we drove onto the ferry that crossed Lake Michigan. We got out of our car and were walking around on the ferry, enjoying the view when two young men came up to us.

"The ferry landing is numerous miles from town. Would you give us a lift?"

"Sure, we'll take you." we said.

As the daylight turned to darkness, with excitement we watched our approach to the distant shore.

A voice announced over the loud speaker, "Everyone back to your cars. Be prepared to disembark." We gathered our hitchhikers and returned to the car.

As the ferry approached the landing the gangplank was lowered. Men in uniform hurried us off of the ship. "Get going! Get going!" they waved each car along. I stomped on the gas pedal, and we roared out of the boat onto a road running along the water's edge. As we bounced off the gang plank I heard a clunk and our car careened toward the edge of the dock, not responding to the steering wheel. We braced ourselves for the plunge into the deep, dark water below.

Then came a loud crunch that threw us forward in our seats. We had fortunately slammed head on into the only iron post on the embankment! Without a word, the young men got out of our car and disappeared.

One Solitary Post

But the car behind us stopped. A man and his wife hurried up to where I crouched under the car, trying to locate what may have caused me to loose control of the steering.

"You must live right or have protecting angels," the man said. " You were headed for the water! It's amazing that you hit the only post along this whole embankment!" He bent down with me and pointed a huge flashlight under our car.

"It looks like the drag link broke," we both said in unison.

"What's that, Eddie?" Milly asked.

Relieved to know what would have taken the lives of our entire family, I explained to Milly, "The bar of metal that connects the steering to the wheel. Do we have a coat hanger?"

"What does Daddy want a coat hanger for, Mummy?" I heard Kevin ask.

"I don't know, darling, but help me find one!" They located one and handed it out the window to me.

I climbed underneath the car and tied the two parts together.

The "Good Samaritan" volunteered, "I'll follow behind you to town where you can get help."

Getting behind the wheel again, I slowly eased our car back from the edge. Then I very slowly drove up the steeply inclined road, gently applying pressure to the gas pedal. Half way up the hill, to my dismay, the coat hanger broke with a bang. Milly prayed, "Jesus! Jesus! Jesus!"

I stomped the brakes, and we jerked to a stop. The man behind us stopped, got out of his car, and handed me a piece of bailing wire that he remembered he had.

Again I climbed back underneath the car and connected the tie rod. The bailing wire held! At the outskirts of Luddington, we slowly inched into the first gas station we came to. Our friends waved goodbye.

The gas station mechanic had already left for the day and would not be back until morning. We had no other choice. We slept in the car.

The following morning, when the station opened, the mechanic looked under our car and diagnosed the problem. "We'll have to go for a new drag link." He wiped his hands with a greasy rag. "It'll be a few hours before you're fixed up."

A few hours wait did not bother us. We were so very grateful not to have been buried in an untimely death in Lake Michigan.

When our car was repaired, we were on the road again. I turned to Milly and assured her, "I think that God is helping us, Milly!"

The countryside was beautiful and unlike anything we'd ever seen. At the top of one of the mountains, we were amused to see a public convenience with a signpost. "London: 5,000 miles, Paris: 6,000 miles, Tokyo: 8,000 miles. Farther down the post was a sign, "Scratching post, men."

A few inches underneath that sign it read," Scratching post, women." A few inches farther down, "Scratching post, kids." Near the ground, a sign read "Scratching post, dogs." And finally a sign, "Scratching post, cats."

We laughed and got the impression that Americans were always ready to see the humor in life and look for the best in everything.

Not only did we drive all day, but often all night. Milly had never been taught how to drive, but she was wonderful company and helped to keep me awake and happy. The children played in the back seat. Periodically, Clive required a diaper change. I then stopped the car by a mountain stream, and Milly did the laundry. She dipped the diapers in the icy water, wrung them out as dry as possible, then clamped them to the outside of the Chevy's rear windows.

We bought our food at grocery stores and prepared it along the way.

The car was also our motel on wheels. The children slept on the back dash, while we stretched out to sleep the best we could on the car seats.

As we drove, we talked about our hopes and dreams. "When we get to Vancouver, we'll find temporary housing, then we'll build our dream house!" I exclaimed enthusiastically. "What do you want in our dream house, Milly?"

"Oh, a yard for the children, and a kitchen with a stove to cook and bake."

"I'll try to get you the most modern stove there is."

"What do you want in a dream house, Eddie?"

"I've always envisioned a white house with a blue roof on a hill overlooking a beautiful view."

"Hmmmmm, certainly does sound like a dream!" Milly said.

At the Montana border, one of the widest states in the union, we were greeted with a huge sign: "Brother, you've got to push a lot of miles behind you to get anyplace in this state."

Although we traveled as fast as we could, it was in Montana that we decided that it wouldn't take much longer to make a side trip once in a while. At one point, we turned south and visited Yellowstone Park. The first things we noticed were the bears and other wild animals. They appeared tame, so we, along with the other tourists, fed the bears quite fearlessly. Kevin even put food directly into their mouths from the window of our car.

Mud pools and holes in the ground bubbled with boiling water. Old Faithful, the park's main geyser, shot thousands of gallons of water into the air at precise moments. We left awed and somewhat frightened at the heat, steam, and geysers that gushed from the very depths of the earth.

The rest of our trip through Montana was uneventful. But in Washington, what a delight! We encountered an unbelievable abundance of delicious fruit: pears, apples, peaches, and apricots. Costing only pennies per pound, it was incredible! We had never seen anything like it!

Finally, we reached Blaine, Washington, the westernmost border crossing into Canada. It was only sixty miles from our longed-for destination, Vancouver. The miles sped by, and soon we entered Vancouver. At that moment, reality hit us. What were we doing here? We knew no one in Vancouver. Where should we go? What should we do first?

I drove to the heart of the city and parked at Victory Square. I did not feel very victorious. The towering buildings made a concrete canyon fourteen stories high.

A policeman knocked on my window and interrupted as I pondered my dilemma. "You aren't allowed to park here for longer than fifteen minutes. Move along!" I started the engine and drove around the square, then parked in a different spot.

"Milly, what have I done to you? Here we sit. I have no idea what to do next. No place to stay. No job. Nothing."

"Eddie, let's pray. You'll soon know what to do. Meanwhile, we're together, and the children are safe, happy, and well fed. The only immediate problem is having to move the car."

I bowed my head. "Thank you, Father, for getting us here safely. Thank you for my wife. Please guide us and show us what to do next."

Clive started to cry. Milly turned to help him, while I looked up at the buildings around us. Many windows had gold lettering naming a business or a service. As I looked up, one sign caught my eye: Department of Veteran's Affairs.

"I'll go talk to them, Milly! Maybe they can help." Of course, it was the Department of Canadian Veterans, but I thought I'd give it a try.

I took the elevator to the correct floor and entered the door marked Veteran's Affairs. The girl at the counter looked up, "Hello, can I be of any help?"

"We've just come over from England. We're down in the park right now, my wife and two children. Do you have any recommendation as to where we can find an inexpensive place to stay until I find a job?"

"Are you Canadian?"

"No, I'm British, but I am a veteran."

"Now let me get this straight," she said. "You've just come from England?"

"Yes."

"You have a wife and children?"

"Yes."

"And you don't know anybody here?"

"That's right."

"Your family is sitting outside in your car?"

"Yes."

"Now? Downstairs? In the park?"

"Yes."

"Well, I must say, you seem to have the courage of your convictions! I don't know if we can help you or not. Let me talk to the superintendent." She disappeared, and I prayed under my breath as I looked out at my family sitting in the car.

The superintendent came out of his inner office. He was a stocky man with a crisp mustache. "The only thing I can do for you is to help you find a hotel. We have a hotel that we've commandeered called the Dunsmuir Hotel, where we are placing Canadian veterans who are in your situation. It would be a single hotel room at a cost of twenty dollars a month. You're not allowed to cook in it, and the facilities are down the hall. But, if that would be of any help to you, I could put you there."

"Thank you," I said. "We very much appreciate it."

I drove Milly and the children to the hotel. It was old, and the facilities were limited. However, instead of one room, they assigned us two! Besides that, although we were told we were not allowed to cook, we learned that everyone had a hot plate and a hidden pan.

Within a few days, I had a job at a tool company making thirty-five dollars a week. In a short time, I was managing my department. However, I did not receive a raise. Watching for a better opportunity, I applied at a typewriter and calculating machine company for better wages. When I was hired, I changed jobs. I was seeing my dreams come true.

A few weeks later a fellow worker told of a beautiful piece of land that had just opened up for development on Vancouver's north shore. I began my first steps to make our dream house come true!

LIFE IN CANADA, 1947–1950

"Milly, dear, I want to give you a little bit of advice," Mrs. Mason had said as we sat in her kitchen, drinking our last cup of tea together. Kevin was playing with some of Graham's old toys, and Clive lay asleep in his stroller. "In Canada, your children's schedules and surroundings will all be changed. To help them adjust, you must keep familiar things around them, for instance, Kevin's favorite toy, and Clive's baby blanket; and wherever you stay, even if it is for only two weeks, make it 'home.'"

Her advice ran through my mind as we emptied our belongings from the car into the Dunsmuir Hotel in Vancouver. I set up pictures on the mantel, my tablecloth on the worn table, and put the packing boxes in the back of the cupboard.

At the grocery store, I found a wilted plant for five cents and nursed it to health. It repaid me by blooming beautifully on the kitchen windowsill. The children's toys were unpacked, and they were given space to play. Each boy had a comforter from England that he knew was his own. I laid each one on his bed. I cooked regular, healthy meals each day. Within a week, the old building was home.

Two weeks after we moved in, I was finishing a letter to Mrs. Mason, thanking her for her advice, when I noticed the boys were unusually quiet. I stepped into the next room and found them with a blanket half out the window.

"Boys! That's a naughty thing to do!" I retrieved the blanket and glanced down at the sidewalk. Angry people stood pointing up at me. At their feet were a dozen toys, a shoe that looked faintly familiar, and an old pan that I had let the boys play with. "Oh, dear!"

I was upset. I raced downstairs, rescued our things and ran back to the boys. "Why did you throw those things down?"

"It made people look up, and the things made noises when they landed!" Kevin said.

"Did the people on the sidewalk look happy?" I asked.

"No, dey didn't, dey looked mad," two-year-old Clive replied.

"And why were they unhappy?"

"Because something could have hit them?" Kevin asked.

"Yes, they could have been hurt badly. And did Mummy look happy when she found you? "

"No, you wasn't," Clive said.

"Why not?"

"'Cause it took time to go and fetch the things?" Kevin asked.

"'Cause dey got dirty?" Clive asked.

"Yes, and someone could have taken our things away, and then we would be missing a shoe, we would be cold at night, and you would have fewer toys! You boys leave the window alone. I will take you to the park to play. All right?"

"All right, Mummy. We're sorry." They hugged me, and we went to make a lunch to take to the park.

We walked hand in hand to the swings. While the boys chased each other up and down the slide, I sat on a nearby bench. A tall lady sat next to me and sent her daughter to the swing. We smiled at each other and talked about the weather.

Out of the blue she asked, "Are you a Christian?"

"Why, yes, I am."

"Where do you attend church?"

"Actually, we haven't found a church yet. We just moved from England."

"I go to the Salvation Army, and you'd sure be welcome if you cared to come." I thanked her and decided to discuss the subject with Eddie that night.

I put the boys to bed early and met Eddie at the door. I deliberately wore my best black skirt and white blouse. I also had cooked a simple stew on the hot plate, serving it as attractively as I could. Eddie seemed to relax as soon as he entered the door.

While we were eating, I mentioned what had happened earlier that day. "We were invited to church next Sunday!"

"What church?"

"The Salvation Army."

"Let's go; maybe they'll have a band I can join." Eddie surprised me, since I thought that I would have difficulty persuading him to attend.

The next Sunday, we drove to the Salvation Army Hall. Sure enough, they had a band and were excited that my husband played the trumpet.

"Do you smoke?" one of the men asked.

"A little," Eddie admitted.

"If you want to play in the band that will have to go."

"So, I'll quit." Eddie replied. Stopping smoking was easy for him. However, two weeks later he returned home from work looking very sick.

"Eddie, what happened? You look green!"

"Ohhh, I feel sick! A buddy offered me a cigarette on the ferry, and I didn't think one would make any difference, so I smoked it." Later that night he declared, "I'll never smoke again if it does this to my body!" And he never did.

We attended the Salvation Army services regularly and wore their uniform. The group was small but very concerned for the salvation of the lost. At one point, we considered attending their training college to become full time workers, but our children would have to be left with strangers while we studied. We chose not to leave them in someone else's care.

One night, after a long day at work, Eddie arrived home with a small chocolate cake, a big smile, and a twinkle in his eye. The cake was a luxury, so I knew something was up. After we ate our meal and had savored every bite of the moist cake, Eddie announced, "I've found the land for our house, Milly!" He pushed his chair away from the table and sat me down on his lap.

"You have?"

"Yes, on the north side of Vancouver. It's on a hill and has a beautiful view of the harbor. On Saturday I'll take you there. We could put the last of our savings that arrived from England as a down-payment on it."

When we were first married, we had stayed at my father's home. After contributing for food and expenses, with Eddie's good sales job, we had been able to save money. However, when we left England, the government allowed us to only bring a small amount. The government also regulated how often subsequent money could be sent to us in Canada.

"I can't wait to see the land that you've found. Please tell me all about it!"

Eddie described in detail the special things he was going to provide. "I even looked at a stove today. You never complain about that hot plate, but I'm going to make it up to you."

On Saturday, Eddie drove with excitement to show me the land. I was not disappointed. It met every requirement of our "dream," so we signed the purchase papers. Following our purchase, Eddie spent his free hours drawing house plans.

"Milly, where do you want your kitchen sink to be? And which room do you think should be the boys' room?"

It was exciting and scary at the same time. We had no experience to guide us. For example, when Eddie asked me what color I wanted the floor to be, I had difficulty visualizing from a tiny sample what carpeting would look like on an entire floor. I just guessed.

Eddie researched and found a contractor who agreed to let us participate in the construction, to keep the costs down. Our dream house was going to require a lot of work and money!

Every week we took a ferry to the north shore and a bus up the hill to our home site. We cleared the land and lay the foundation, then framed our home. Finally, came the roof, followed by walls and the drywall.

As we worked diligently on the construction, the boys were always with us. They explored and played in the mud and springtime slush. We thought we always knew where they were. However, one day a woman walked our boys over to us.

"I found these two in my garden, breaking my decorations," she asserted angrily and touched the shoulders of the two sheepish boys. I climbed down from the scaffold and apologized profusely.

After she left, I took the boys over to the steps. "Now, boys, explain this to me." They proceeded to tell of the fun that they'd just had. "Did the lady have fun breaking her things with you?"

"'Course not," Clive admitted.

"The Bible says, 'do unto others the way you want them to do to you.' Would you like someone to come along and start breaking our house?"

"No, but we didn't bwake her house, and our yard is already bwoken!" Clive said.

"What about when our yard is all fixed, then how would you like it?"

"Wouldn't like it," Kevin said.

"She's going to be one of our neighbors. Was it smart to hurt her things when we are trying to be friendly and get to know her as a neighbor?"

"Guess not." Kevin put his head down. "I'm sorry. Are we going to get a spank?"

"Yes, and why do you think I'm going to spank you?" I asked sadly.

"To help us 'member'?" Clive said.

"Yes, to help you to remember." So I turned each one over on my knee and gave one smack with my hand on each bottom. Then we hugged and changed the subject to a positive note.

"I tell you what," I interjected, "You made a mistake today, but next time you're going to use your smart little heads better, aren't you? Daddy and I have been really pleased with how you've helped us move rocks and branches and picked up nails. And before long, you're going to get a reward for all that work."

"A reward?" both of them dropped little jaws, and their eyes got big.

"Yes, a bicycle each!"

"I can't be happy about it yet, " Kevin stated dejectedly.

"Why is that, son?"

"Because I didn't say 'sorry' to the neighbor yet."

I wiped their cheeks clean, then watched as they went hand in hand to the neighbor's front door. I saw the door open and the lady lean over to listen. She gave them each a hug as they disappeared into her home. A few minutes later, they each ran back to us with cookies in hand. Kevin could now be happy.

At the end of the day, we collected and locked up the tools.

"Hurry boys! You can finish that fort you're making tomorrow. We've got to catch the last bus."

We ran down the hill to the bus exhausted and dirty. After the ferry ride, we tumbled into the car, drove back to the Dunsmuir Hotel, and dragged ourselves up the steps of the hotel. Our dreams were very hard work!

During this exciting time, I had a big surprise to share with Eddie, so I bought a chocolate cake for our evening's dessert. As we ate it, I asked Eddie, "Do you know what we are celebrating?"

"That you're the most beautiful, wonderful woman in the world?"

"No, Eddie, I'm serious!"

"I am serious!" he hugged me and sat me on his lap. "That the framing on the house is done?"

"No, I'm glad about that, but that's not it," I said.

"The children haven't thrown anything out of the window for a long time?"

"No, Eddie! It's another miracle. We're going to have a baby!"

He turned pale. "Are you quite sure?"

"Quite sure!" I replied emphatically.

"I've been thinking about babies lately," he admitted. "Actually, I've been thinking that if we should ever have another child, it would be nice if it were a girl. Wouldn't you think so? My coming home to you and our two precious little boys, to a white house with a blue roof and a big picture window overlooking Vancouver's Howe Sound, and to add the cherry to the top of the dessert, a baby girl. I was pleased that not only did he like my dessert, but my happy announcement as well.

Eddie worked part time doing photography, along with his full time tool sales job to save money for a newer car. After a year of incredibly hard physical labor, we moved out of the hotel and into our dream house.

The house was not quite finished, but we wanted to be settled in before the baby arrived. As we were moving in and unpacking, the church ladies brought gifts for our home, including a set of fine English bone china. I was thrilled. The men of the church also brought Eddie a wheelbarrow full of tools.

In the meantime, Eddie's brother, followed by his parents, had moved to Canada from England, so Grandmother Ware came to visit and help us move in. On April 22, 1950, Eddie helped admit me to the hospital. He then returned home with his mother and the boys to wait for the birth announcement.

A few hours later, a nurse called from the hospital, "Mr. Ware, your wife just had a baby."

"Oh! Yes! How wonderful! And what was it?" he queried.

" A ba . . . by . . ."

"Yes! Yes! A baby. But what kind of baby?" he interrupted impatiently.

"Well, Mr. Ware, a baby," she said slowly, "a baby girl!" Eddie broke into happy tears.

Months later, we were sitting on our new furniture in the living room. The drape was pulled back to enjoy the lights from the harbor through our big picture window. The boys were asleep, and I had just put Heather into her crib. As I snuggled next to Eddie, he put his arm around me, but I sensed that something was bothering him. I asked, "What's on your mind, Eddie?"

"It seems like a never-ending quest, always striving for better things. What I thought were perfect house plans, aren't. What I thought would completely satisfy me, hasn't. There are things about the neighbor's new houses that I like better than ours."

"But, Eddie," I protested, "I'm really enjoying our house! The stove is wonderful, along with everything else. I think you've done a tremendous job, and I thank you for it!" I put my arms around him and hugged him. "You've worked so hard and have really done well."

We sat in silence, each thinking our own thoughts. Then I reminded him, "Remember when we were kids and gave our lives to serve God? Maybe God doesn't want us to get so satisfied that we forget our promise."

Eddie sat up agitated. "If He wants me to do something, He's got to make it really clear. Right now I'm working on First Timothy 5: 8."

I went over to my Bible to find the verse that he referred to. I read, "If any provide not for his own and specially for those of his own house, he hath denied the faith, and is worse than an infidel."

Despite Eddie's dissatisfaction, we continued to improve our home and increase our home furnishings from week to week. Also, our children gave us great joy. Both Eddie and

I agreed that life was very good. We continued to attend church and found that some of our neighbors were also Christians.

One neighbor rode the ferry to work with Eddie. He and his wife constantly entertained missionaries and ministers, and they often invited us to come to their home to meet them.

One night, I stayed home with the children while Eddie went next door to meet a guest minister. The minister was talking about demons. He said that he could see them in the room as they crawled around.

Eddie hurried home that night. "I'm not going back, Milly! That was weird, and I didn't appreciate it. Where does it say anything in the Bible about demons crawling around, I'd like to know!" We both shivered at the thought.

Months went by. Again our neighbor came to invite us to a Christian gathering at his home. He turned to Eddie. "It's nothing like that other time. This person is a missionary and talks straight on the Bible. I think that you'd really enjoy him!"

"I've got work to do," Eddie replied. "I can watch the children if Milly wants to go."

"All right, I'll go," I said, since I couldn't think of an excuse. "What time is the meeting?"

"Seven o'clock. Look forward to seeing you," he said, and walked down the driveway.

The guest speaker that night was Paul Flemming, a missionary. From the moment he opened his mouth, I was riveted. At the end of his talk, he challenged each one of us to serve God on the mission field. Turning to me he asked, "What about you?"

"I'm married with three children!" I protested.

"That's no excuse. God wants to use you."

Around midnight, when I arrived home, I woke Eddie. "You won't believe this! You've just simply got to hear this man! He's presented a challenge to me that I think is of the Lord. You've got to go tomorrow night."

He grunted. "That's nice. Tell me about it in the morning." Eddie rolled over and went back to sleep.

As I went to bed, I wondered how I could get Eddie to go hear what I heard? I fell asleep with an idea that I hoped would work.

The memory of the previous night was lost in the morning rush, but when Eddie returned from work, I was at the door wearing my favorite dress. The aroma of roast with all the trimmings filled the house. I kissed him and handed Heather to him. She was fed, bathed, and in her cutest dress. Eddie carried the baby with him into our bedroom, and I held my breath. I was praying that my plan would work. I had laid his going-out-clothes on the bed. They were ironed and ready to put on.

"Where we going, 'Ange'?" Eddie called out, using his abbreviation for "Angel," which he often called me.

"What I told you about last night, darling. It's your turn tonight!" I announced as if he were going to pick out a free Rolls Royce or something equally as desirable.

"What are you talking about? Maybe I don't want to go out tonight. Maybe I just want to stay home and snuggle with my beautiful wife," he responded. He was silent for a few moments. "You don't want me to go to the neighbor's, do you?"

"Oh, please, dear. It was so good. I want you to hear what I heard! Please go, just for me." I came up and kissed him.

"All right, I guess I could go. But if it's anything like the last time, I'll leave before it starts."

"Oh, thank you! It isn't anything like the last time. Thank you, thank you!" I was overjoyed with gratitude for the answer to my prayer.

As soon as supper was over, he played with the boys, then headed for the door.

The neighbor's house was lit up, and there were a dozen cars parked in front. I watched and prayed as Eddie knocked on their door. I saw that he was cordially welcomed, so I closed the drape and got the children ready for bed. Hours passed. A few minutes before eleven o'clock, I checked the window. Cars were still parked at the neighbor's house.

Preparing for bed, I dropped to my knees and prayed, "Dear God, thank You for the privilege of being Yours, and for all that You have done for us. If You have plans for Eddie and me, please make them very clear, and help us to do whatever you desire." With that, I got into bed and began to read. I had fallen asleep when, about midnight, Eddie woke me up! He was standing by the bed looking at me. The last time I had seen that look on his face was when we were teenage sweethearts, and we had given our lives to serve God.

"God has everything, Milly! Everything! The only thing that God doesn't have is us! The value of one soul saved is worth more than the entire world!" He sat on the edge of the bed. "If one person is of such value, then what are we doing wasting our energy worrying what color our bathroom is?" He hardly stopped to take a breath. "Last year a plane-load of missionaries crashed in Venezuela. They all died. God has to replace those Christian soldiers. Are you willing to leave everything and fill their place?"

"It scares me a little, Eddie, but yes, I'll step out in faith with you. I wonder what God wants to do with us?"

"I'm not sure, but I believe that we need to be found faithful right now. About the Father's business."

The next day, we called a few families we knew and started a meeting in our home to pray for the mission field, both in our neighborhood and around the world. God unusually blessed our meetings so that more people came each week. Soon there were several dozen who attended. Shortly after, we sent money to various missions, especially Brother Flemming's.

After almost a year, we received a letter:

Dear Fellow Workers,

We have received letters from so many Canadian candidates for the missionary field that we have decided to start a training school, or boot camp, in Canada. Would you consider heading that up, as we see that you are leading the group there already?

Signed,
Paul Flemming

We called a meeting to discuss the challenge presented in Paul's letter. The oldest couple in our group said, "We couldn't do that. We're too old. We would be much more productive as prayer warriors, backing up those that feel led to go out. We cannot go."

Each person had a reason for not getting involved. One young man who had already been a missionary but had married a non-Christian said, "My heart burns within me, but I can't consider it. My wife is already upset that I attend these house meetings. I cannot go."

"That leaves us," Eddie decided.

We were excited at the thought of serving God.

One valued friend told us that there were three steps in knowing God's will. The first: Is it Scriptural? The second:

Do you have a desire to do it? The third: Do the circumstances work out? If it is His will, He will make it possible.

A week later, a man whom we'd never seen before, knocked on our door. "I've been looking at your house for the last month. If you should ever want to sell it, please let me know."

Shortly after, another letter arrived from Paul Flemming:

Dear Fellow Workers,

There is a plane-load of twenty-six missionary candidates flying to the mission field. I will be among them. If you arrange a meeting, we could make a stop there for a night. To hear missionaries trained and ready to go out first hand could be a real boost to the work.

Signed,
Paul Flemming

We were excited and called our group together to discuss how we should arrange for this meeting.

One person suggested, "Let's rent the sports arena of the Pacific National Exhibition Grounds and invite the whole city!" Another suggested, "No, let's get one of our small local churches, perhaps yours or ours, and have a small gathering of those that we think might be interested."

I said, "No, the exhibition grounds are a little bit over-ambitious, and yet I think we could do better than just a small church of forty or fifty people." We sought the cooperation of the pastor of a large church and found him only too happy to help us.

We advertised and looked forward to this special occasion. The mission sent a man named Leroy Larson to help us prepare. He was to answer any questions and help with the gathering.

The night before the event, we received a telephone call from Paul Flemming, "We are running really behind on our schedule, so we cannot make it up to Canada. Carry on with the meeting. Brother Larson will help, and we'll pray that it will be a real blessing."

We were deeply disappointed, since we had looked forward to hearing Mr. Flemming again.

Eddie groaned. "The people are expecting someone important and all they'll get is us!"

The next night the building was filled to capacity and people were turned away at the door. The service proceeded with joyous and challenging testimonies and songs. As I listened, Kevin and Clive on each side of me and the baby on my lap, I worried about our children's well being. If Eddie quit work and we lived by faith, would our children get what they needed: food, shelter, and education? During the meeting, I confessed my fears to God, and by faith, entrusted our children to His care.

After the meeting, many desired to stay for prayer. It was after midnight when we returned home.

The next morning, as we sat at the breakfast table, Eddie flipped on the radio to hear the day's news and weather. "There has been an airplane crash in the United States. A plane with twenty-six missionaries ran into the Grand Tetons. All aboard are believed dead."

Eddie looked at me in horror. Our eyes registered disbelief, then dumb shock. "Could it be . . . How could it not be . . . Paul Flemming and the others were twenty-six!"

A telephone call proved that the report was accurate. The very group of missionaries that we had expected, all perished on the side of a cold mountain. Why?

"The Lord allows some to go, so that many more will take their place," echoed in my mind from the words of Paul

Flemming, when he told us with passion about the airplane accident in Venezuela years before.

We spent many days in shock, praying and grieving. The Lord answered our prayers by giving Eddie a poem: the need and vision was to live in our hearts.

We Die if You Delay

Have you ever heard the pleading that calls from o'er the sea,
The cry of dying millions, to the heart of you and me?
We hardly hear the words above the din of life,
Yet with dawning comprehension, they stab me like a knife.

They rise from the poor, deprived, and banned.
They come with no less agony from the richest in the land.
From tormented souls of prisoners behind bars,
Their cries ascend unheeded and lonely to the stars.

From sophisticated cities, with chic, opulent styles,
To the frozen tundra of the north, and south to golden isles.
The call comes ringing I cannot say it nay.
It beckons, "Come, we need you. We die if you delay."

We continue to sit indifferent, complacent in our ease.
Our head upon a pillow, a book upon our knees.
What if the reverse were true,
We were enslaved, and they were me and you?

We must focus our attention, to our flesh resist.

Set our heart upon obedience and on it insist.
Go and tell of our Lord Jesus, His mercy, love, and
grace,
Proclaim His glorious message to every single race.

We walked around in a sad daze for days, and many times tears rolled down our cheeks. One morning, after Eddie had gone to work, I was on my knees crying for the loved ones of those who had died. Clive came in and knelt beside me. "Why are you crying, Mummy?"

"Because we're going to miss our Christian brothers and sisters who died."

"Where did they go, Mummy?"

"They went to be with Jesus. They're talking with Jonah and Elijah, whom we read about last night."

Clive interrupted, "And will they see the little boy who gave Jesus his fish?"

"Yes, and all the disciples, and Grandmother Halliday, and . . ." As Clive and I continued to compile the list, I realized that those who had gone before were the privileged ones. With Clive's questions, I was comforted.

Eddie was so certain that God had called us, he proceeded to plan for the missionary training camp. An Assemblies of God church offered the use of their church summer camp to open our training camp.

We desired to go forward unencumbered and not have ties to entice us back. So we burned our bridges by selling and giving away the belongings that we would not need as missionaries. I only saved two things. One was the set of china dishes that the Salvation Army ladies had given us as a housewarming gift. The luxury of having those expensive dishes from my former home country warmed my heart each time I used them. The other was our mattress. Eddie and I had sacrificed for a long time to pay for it. Since I would have missed it terribly, we decided to take it with us. Surely the God that said He "giveth His beloved sleep" knew that I needed it. And surely He looked at what I gave up, not what I hung on to!

Many people questioned our sanity. "You've got a family and responsibilities. How can you throw your job, your new home, your friends, and all that you've worked for to the wind? You're going to regret what you're doing and come back penniless, begging us to take you in."

All that we could say was, "We'll never know unless we try. God left Heaven to come to earth to save us. The Bible says in Matthew 16:25, 'For whosoever will save his life shall lose it: and whosoever will lose his life for my sake shall find it'."

MISSIONARY BOOT CAMP, 1951–1953

"God listens to young people's promises," Milly said as we drove over the rough logging roads to join the men and women dedicated to founding a missionary training camp. "God did not forget our promise at age fourteen that we would be missionaries, did He?"

"Why do you think we didn't become missionaries back then?" I asked.

Milly thought for a moment. "I think God wanted to train us first, me in nursing, and you with mechanical things."

I expanded on the thought, "I think He had to show us that living for Him is more fulfilling than living for ourselves. If we had 'left everything,' before we had anything to leave, we might have wondered at some point what we had missed." The forest around us got thicker as the gravel road turned into ruts and potholes.

"Where are we going to live, Daddy?" Kevin asked.

"We're going to stay in a big building with other families, and then we hope to build cabins in the woods."

"Why will we stay with other families?" Clive asked.

"Because we have to learn to love one another and work together as the family of God."

I started to think about a conversation that Milly and I had had the night before. "Milly, you and I have chosen to live by faith, but our children have no choice. They may suffer."

It had been our last night in the warmth of our home. "Eddie, if God cannot take care of our children, then He is not the God we think He is."

At last we arrived at the primitive camp, and I parked our loaded car near a small building. It was springtime and wild flowers bloomed everywhere. Our children jumped out of the car and started to pick handfuls. Milly soon had several bouquets and rummaged through our things for a container. "Go to the stream and fill this cup with water to put the flowers in," Milly said as she sent the children skipping off.

That night, all of the recruits gathered and prayed, "Lord, here we are. We believe that you have guided us, and we pray that we will learn quickly, so that we can be sent out to the field that is 'white unto harvest.'"

In the months that followed, we read and studied the Bible as a group on the grounds of the summer camp. Leroy Larson, the man who had been sent earlier by Paul Flemming, stayed as our camp leader. Many years before, he had been a missionary and was struck down with polio. Now he taught us the Bible from his wheelchair. Those who were able, worked together to improve the campgrounds, and we all learned to understand and love each other. The atmosphere was alive with the novelty and excitement of training to become physically, spiritually, and psychologically ready for the rigors of foreign mission work.

One major challenge was the camp's water system. A stream, diverted into pipes above the camp, ran to a huge water tank. The water tank, or cistern, was made of giant pieces of sewer pipe, six feet across and four feet deep. Three sections were stacked to a height of twelve feet. When the tank was full, it provided enough pressure for the water to reach the faucets and toilets. During the previous winter, the top two sections of six-inch thick pipe had frozen and cracked.

I reviewed the problem aloud to Milly one night as we prepared for bed. "How can I keep the tank full, so it maintains enough pressure? I can't apply cement to the outside of the crack because the water pressure will push it out. The repair must be inside the tank, where the water itself can work for me." A light clicked on in my head. "Some roofing felt placed against the crack on the inside should just do the trick." Excited and pleased with myself at this inspiration, I could hardly wait for morning.

After breakfast, I asked one of the other men to help me climb to the top of the enormous cistern, to lower a four-by-six foot piece of felt paper down into the water. We carefully maneuvered it into place over the crack. Presto! It worked perfectly! We sat on the top of the rim, twelve feet above the ground, and watched the water gradually creep up inside.

"You're a genius, Ware, an absolute genius!" my cohort exclaimed. I had to admit I did feel proud of myself.

"I wonder what else needs improving in the camp?" I asked my new friend. We were discussing various problems, when I happened to notice that the crack had widened! The water had built up and was exerting enormous pressure on the crack.

"Isn't that crack widening?" I asked.

My friend glanced at what we thought we had fixed. "Well, I believe it is!"

The obvious solution was to remove the piece of felt quickly. However, no matter how hard we pulled on the piece of felt, we could not remove it. It was lodged in the crack.

I nervously suggested, "Well, uhm, I think maybe we'd better get out of here!" We jumped, and in the same instant, the enormous top pipe shattered into a dozen pieces, raining huge chunks of cement down around us. Miraculously, we were not hit, but we did get soaked as several thousand gallons of water cascaded through the camp, causing a minor flood.

Sheepishly, my friend and I made our way to the camp director. "There's been a slight accident, and uhm, well, uhm, the water tank burst, and . . ." We thought that he would dismiss us on the spot, but instead he commented nonchalantly, "We'll just have to put up with low water pressure."

His easygoing manner surprised us. We breathed a sigh of relief. The tank was never repaired but my cocky attitude was. I thought long and hard about how I had nearly killed us both. I thanked God for protecting my helper and me and prayed that my attitude of self-sufficiency and bravado would mellow into a quiet spirit. I learned that God doesn't value the strong and capable, but the yielded weak, through whom He can be strong. Our strengths can only be useful to God if they are yielded to Him. As Hudson Taylor, the great missionary to China, said: "God chose me because I was weak enough. God does not do His great works by large committees. He trains somebody to be quiet enough, and little enough, and then He uses him."

I was learning so much about God and myself that each day was an adventure and time flew by. A few months later, seventy acres of woodland near Enderby, B.C., was donated to the mission. It had no electricity, sewer, or water.

"This is perfect," I exulted to Milly, "exactly what we need. A place where we can learn to work in primitive conditions, just as we'll find on the mission field."

"We are nearly out of money, Eddie," Milly reminded me quietly.

"By the time we help buy the tools we need to build cabins, we will be broke. And won't that be wonderful! We can start to really live by faith!" I declared enthusiastically.

Milly glanced over at our three sleeping children and down at her rounded tummy; then she gave me a hug and agreed, "We will trust the Lord."

Before we left the Assembly of God summer camp, all the men went to work at the donated property, to prepare it for housing for our families. I noticed that daily we passed lumber mills and logging camps that I had earlier visited as an office equipment repairman.

I suggested to the man next to me, "I could stop in and offer to repair some of their equipment. They normally have to wait for months for a serviceman to come to them from Vancouver."

"Maybe you could barter for lumber," he added.

After we arrived at the mission site, we set up a large tent in a clearing. I offered to cook eggs and hash for our supper. As we ate, we sat around a log fire discussing our building plans.

During one of the days that followed, I found time to visit a local wood mill. I informed the foreman, "I am an office equipment repairman. Do you have need of my services?"

"What will it cost us?" the concerned foreman asked.

"How about some wood? We're building cabins and could use your seconds."

"That's a wonderful deal. You fix our equipment, and you can have all the wood you need!" I carried my tools from the car and immediately repaired a broken typewriter. When I returned to camp with the good news, all of the men rejoiced at God's provision.

We worked around the clock, building cabins and digging holes for outhouses. As soon as our cabin was built, Milly and the children and I moved in. We relied on primitive, basic survival skills: going to the river for water, using candlelight, and going to bed early. We planted a garden but ran out of food before the vegetables were edible. We prayed. A local farmer stopped by our mission to see what all the pounding and banging was. He observed our building skills and offered to compensate us if we built him a cabin on his property. This brought in food money!

Each family was individually responsible for its financial income and spending. The purpose was to simulate living by faith for individual needs on the missionary field. Some candidates were supported by their home churches; others had access to personal savings and income; some lived hand-to-mouth from one gift to the next. However, one young couple received a money gift. They very unwisely bought filet mignon steaks and caviar with it! Later that same week, all their money was gone!

During the fall of our first year, none of us had money for meat. One of the men was desperate. "I've got to have some meat!" he announced and initiated a hunting expedition.

"Are you coming, Ware?"

"No, I promised Farmer O'Henry that I would finish his outhouse."

"He's been without an outhouse for twenty years. An extra few days won't hurt him any."

"I guess not, but I want him to learn to trust my word, so he'll start to believe the Word, which I've been telling him about."

"Your choice." They each left to prepare for the hunt.

Farmer O'Henry was so grateful for my help on his outhouse that he rewarded me with a quarter of a deer! When the missionary candidates arrived back from their hunting trip two days later empty-handed, they passed our cabin. They saw the quarter of deer hanging from our porch. The leader of the hunting expedition told me, "The Lord must have approved of your choice!"

We continued our rigorous work schedule. After a few months of intense effort, we finished the construction of the camp: fourteen cabins, four outhouses, and a chapel.

During mid-winter, when Milly was due to deliver our fourth child, we drove to a doctor in the nearest town. Dr. Kope was sympathetic to our mission. When he delivered our beautiful daughter, Lorraine Joy, on December 9, 1951, he insisted that we owed him nothing. Our cup was full and running over with joy!

Later, on May 12, 1953, we returned to him for the delivery of our fifth child. As we held Gleason Paul in our arms, we thrilled at God's grace in our lives. We recalled that Milly had been told that she could not have children. Each of our five children was a special gift. Again, Dr. Kope donated his services. To show her gratitude to the doctor, Milly gave Mrs. Kope her cherished English bone china.

I asked Milly, "Why did you give your china away?"

"Because it meant too much to me. On the mission field I need durable dishes, ones that won't make me sad if they break."

We no longer had beautiful dishes, but we ate well from the garden. Although our menu was limited, it was nutritious. Milly baked delicious loaves of crusty bread to complement our meals of corn chowder, soups, stews, beans, and brawn (the jelly that comes from cooking, then cooling bones). During this time of food scarcity, we taught our children, "Waste not, want not." Waste not included even the smallest crust of bread.

However, from time to time there was an abundance of only one vegetable. For example, one season there was a bumper crop of turnips. We ate turnips until I begged, "Milly, please have the women plant some other vegetable. I can't stand another bite of turnip!"

Another season, it was squash. We ate boiled squash, fried squash, hidden squash, mashed squash. Yuck! Squash!

We learned also to expect the unexpected. One night, someone pounded on our cabin door. When we opened it, a distant neighbor nearly fell into the house. "Help me! Please come and help me!" he gasped. "My wife is having a baby. She's having trouble," he stammered, out of breath from running.

Milly looked at me for my approval, then grabbed her coat and ran out into the bitterly cold night. The man's old pickup truck sped down the snow-covered country road. When Milly arrived, the woman was indeed in trouble and too far along to be taken to a doctor.

The farmer's home revealed heartbreaking poverty. Quickly, Milly surveyed the scene and planned her strategy. First, her patient, who had already been in labor for ten hours, was a cooperative, down-to-earth woman; second, the father was a frightened, emotional man with false teeth continually clacking.

Milly turned to him, "Please get wood for the stove. We have to sterilize a bed sheet to put the baby on."

While he was outside, she found a string wrapped around the top of a bag of flour. She removed the string from the bag and sterilized it in some boiling water, to tie the umbilical cord.

As the sun rose the next morning, the baby started to come. To Milly's dismay, the baby was in a membrane-like sac. As she removed the sac, to her horror, she discovered that the baby boy had a harelip, a severe cleft palate, and its face was flat. Milly looked up at the father who was watching her. His face turned ashen. She wrapped the baby carefully in the sterile sheet. Turning to the patient, Milly was alarmed to see that the woman had started to hemorrhage. She laid the infant in his father's arms and worked to save the mother. By 8:00 A.M., the snowstorm had passed. Milly felt safe to bundle her patients into the pickup truck to drive to the doctor in town.

"I can do nothing for your child," the doctor sorrowfully informed them. "He will live only a short time." The devastated parents took the baby home. They fed him with an eyedropper throughout the day and night, until he died at three months. Following his death, the farmer came and banged again on our door, his hat in his hands. "Would you make a coffin and bury our baby?"

"Of course, we will. We'll be over as soon as it is morning." I got up early and made a casket of clear pine lumber. Milly and I helped to give the sweet little fellow a proper Christian burial under a lone pine on a hill on the farmer's property.

A few days later, the farmer appeared at our door again. "How much do I owe you?"

"Oh, you don't owe us anything. We do this for Jesus. We don't charge anything."

"Well, I've got to pay you somehow." He appeared a little nervous, and his teeth started to chatter. "I know," he said, a light coming to his eyes, "I'll deliver milk, eggs, and butter every week, and sometimes other things, but always eggs, milk, and butter."

Our heart ached for the man. I could hardly speak for the lump in my throat and for holding back tears as he patted my baby's head and left for home. What a blessing he was to us as we saw our children thrive with the nourishing food he lovingly brought.

Some time later, Milly was alarmed by Kevin and Clive's cries. "Mummy! Come quickly! Heather's hurt!" Kevin and Clive announced one afternoon. Milly grabbed Joy under one arm and Paul under the other and ran after them.

"Where is she?"

"We were climbing up on the water truck, and she followed us. Her hand is stuck on the hooks on the side of the truck."

Reaching the central clearing, Milly could see Heather screaming and thrashing her free arm and legs as she hung, impaled by her right hand, from the side of the tall truck.

I also heard Heather's screams from the other side of camp where I was at a Bible study and came running. As I lifted Heather, Milly gently slid her hand off the hook. She wiped the blood off to see the extent of the damage and observed sadly, "It's got to have stitches." We tried to soothe Heather as we drove to the doctor's office.

Following this painful accident, Heather accidentally set fire to our cabin. The fire did little damage to the cabin, but Heather's right leg was severely burned. Milly applied first-aid compresses while the entire camp assembled to pray for her. I held her until she fell into an exhausted sleep, then knelt by her bed, praying until daybreak. To our delight, Heather wakened early, singing, the gauze from the bandage trailing behind her as she walked effortlessly around the room with her doll. God had healed her. Hallelujah!

As our family grew, we built a larger cabin out of the same unfinished tongue-and-groove siding. We packed sawdust between the exterior and the inner walls for insulation, running the stovepipe through the insulation to the outside. During very cold weather, we kept the stove burning all the time. One morning, Milly saw smoke and then a flame coming through the wall. She rushed the children outside into the freezing air, shouting, "Fire! Fire!" Our friends ran from all directions, slipping on the icy ground as they carried buckets of water. Through team effort, they were able to extinguish the flames. The cabin was not destroyed. We were able to move back into the cabin the same night. After that incident, we were more cautious, not allowing the stove and stovepipe to get too hot.

Milly always amazed me with her unflinching courage and willingness to endure hardships. Her positive attitude was a constant inspiration to me as well as to others. She washed our clothes on a washboard in the cabin and then hung them out to dry, or freeze, if it was winter. Believe it or not, stained cloth diapers whiten when they freeze–some comfort when you are out of diapers and need a dry one to diaper a baby!

Not only were we involved in food and shelter survival for our children, but we were also supportive of their education. Kevin and Clive attended a school in the nearby town. They had to walk about a mile to catch the bus. Sometimes they noted wistfully that their school friends used special lunch pails, and their sandwiches were wrapped in plastic. We could not give them these luxuries, but they certainly never went hungry for food or love.

In addition to our caring for our family, some of our training required visiting neighbors and sharing God's love. Milly chose to go to the homes of neighboring farmers. "Eddie, it was disgusting," she said when she returned. "The first farmer I visited with is living with a woman who is not his wife, and worse yet, it doesn't even bother him. I stopped at another home that smelled so bad that I held my nose as I knocked on the door. An old woman invited me in, but her place was such a mess I couldn't sit down. Come to find out, she's a retired teacher! She looks like a witch!"

"Milly, on the mission field you'll see a lot worse. God came to save sinners, not perfect people."

Our camp leader, Leroy Larson, preparing us for our mission, often taught from the book of Romans. He emphasized the grace of God. Among us were Baptists, Methodists,

Presbyterians, Catholics, Mennonites, and Pentecostals. Mr. Larson always avoided controversial issues, and no one was allowed to proselytize other group members to his church doctrines. We were all there with the goal of bringing men and women to a personal commitment to God.

During these sessions, one issue that did precipitate a lot of discussion, however, was the "fall-aways" (those that believed that you could lose your salvation by your behavior, or lack of it) versus "once-and-for-alls" (those that believed that you could not lose your salvation no matter what).

To address this issue, Mr. Larson read Romans 3:10, "There is none righteous, no, not one".

Then he asked us to turn to Romans 3:23–24: "For all have sinned and come short of the glory of God; being justified freely by His grace through the redemption that is in Christ Jesus". Romans 4:16: "Therefore it is of faith, that it might be by grace . . . "; and Romans 5:20, "But where sin abounded, grace did much more abound: that as sin hath reigned unto death, even so might grace reign through righteousness unto eternal life by Jesus Christ our Lord". As Milly left the early morning study session, she walked with her sons to their bus stop. On the way back, she was reviewing the lesson of God's grace. Suddenly it hit her, "It's all finished! I don't have to work for it. I'm not going to lose my salvation!" she sang out to the trees around her. My dear little wife then admitted that she danced joyously, right in the middle of the road!

One day I arrived home from a day's work and found Milly beaming from ear to ear. "Remember that woman I called a witch? I took her a hot loaf of bread today. She let me in and shared some of her past experiences. No wonder she's a recluse! Before I left, we cried and prayed together."

A week later, I went with Milly to visit the old woman and found a tidy place and a happy lady. After her counseling session with Milly, her life had turned around. Her home was clean and neat, and she was completely changed. Her countenance radiated joy and peace.

I also met the man "living in sin" that Milly had told me about. I saw him walking down our road. "What's happened to your wife?" he asked.

"What do you mean?"

"I mean that she's changed! The first time she visited us, she was about to pray fire and brimstone down on me and my woman. Now she's almost convinced me to get married, and she hasn't even brought the subject up."

I could see that the training was working. We were all becoming more like Christ, and miracles happened. As time passed, some of our candidates felt they were ready, and left for their mission field.

One of the candidates who left, Paul Gifford, had visited our cabin often. A vibrant Christian, he left us to work with the American branch of our mission camp in California. Soon after, we received a letter saying that he had died while fighting a forest fire. "What an incredible loss to the work of God," I mourned. "How I look forward to the day when we meet again in a better place."

After eighteen months in the Canadian boot camp, we also moved to the mission camp in northern California. A long, dusty road led to the camp. Rows of cabins, an airstrip, a store, and a school for the children sat huddled among the tall green pines. My assignment was to teach building skills with other survival strategies, and Milly was given charge of the infirmary.

Soon after our arrival, one young candidate fell from a telephone pole and was brought to Milly unconscious. Deciding that his case required immediate medical attention, she decided to rush him to the nearest doctor one hundred miles away. We prayed all the way. When we arrived with the unconscious patient, the doctor started to stitch up the gash on his head. As the doctor was stitching, the young man regained consciousness. He confronted the doctor: "Are you going to hell or heaven, Doctor?"

Shaken and unsure how he should respond, the physician asked, "Is he always like this, or is he irrational?"

"He's always like that," we assured him. Since the doctor found no other problems, we drove him back to camp rejoicing.

Milly had another life-and-death challenge that many women fear. Sheryl Flemming, the widow of Paul Flemming, came to Milly, having discovered lumps in her breasts. She was prayed for, but a few weeks later, she reported that the lumps were no smaller. We were all very concerned and encouraged her to consult a physician. Milly accompanied her to Sacramento, where the doctors decided that they would remove the lumps, examine them for cancer, and then proceed according to the diagnosis.

On the day of surgery, the surgeon discovered that the lumps were most unusual, so much so that he called in another doctor for a second opinion. "Look at this! I've never seen lumps like this before! They're all sort of dying from inside out." The lumps had atrophied and had shriveled! Milly was jubilant with this unexpected report.

Many experienced missionaries challenged us. They shared how they were able to meet impossible obstacles by faith. When one candidate left us to go to Venezuela, the Venezuelan immigration office refused him entry into their country. "Nobody needs you here," the administrator said, "unless your religion can help my brother. He is in the insane institution. If you can help him, I will sign the permission for you to stay."

The missionary had never dealt with mental problems before, so he stepped aside and prayed. "What shall I do?"

The promise of God's Word came to his mind: "By my stripes you are healed." On the strength of that promise, he bowed his head and prayed out loud for the man's brother.

A week later, the missionary returned to the immigration office. When he entered, the administrator called him over to his window. "My brother is home again! The doctors cannot explain why he is better, so it must be your prayer. You may enter my country. We need you."

Another one of our candidates went to Sumatra. She, too, was forbidden entry into the nation that she felt called to. Day after day she sat on the doorstep of the government building, until the officials tired of seeing her there.

"If you want to go into the jungles so bad, go!" they said.

So she went with only a tiny native woman for company. One day she became very ill with dysentery; she longed for only a piece of bread. The native woman companion had gone into the village and was walking past a Dutch official who had traveled there. Unexpectedly, he gave her a loaf of bread! The companion didn't even know what it was, but she returned to the missionary and gave the gift to her.

The missionary, Kathy Hawthorne, wrote home: "God knew that I was in the jungles, desperately wanting something from home, and the Lord put it in the jungles for me!"

Before Kathy left for Sumatra, she was invited to speak to one hundred students at nine o'clock each morning for a week. However, she was suffering with a severe case of laryngitis and could only make a whistling sound. Miraculously, at nine o'clock each morning, the Lord restored her voice. She spoke for an hour, and when she was through, her voice was gone again.

All of these people and their testimonies strongly influenced our lives. We realized that nothing is impossible with God. Nothing! We can trust Him, depend on Him, love Him, and believe Him for anything.

Following an exciting year in California, we were asked to return to the camp in Canada. At the Canadian border, an officer asked to search our car. Milly had just changed Paul's diaper, and I had gingerly placed it in the back to be washed later. When I opened up the back of the car, the officer took one whiff and said, "That's all right, just go ahead!"

Back in Canada at the camp in Enderby, I was assigned to travel all over Canada, recruiting men and women to become missionaries. On one occasion, a Christian lady who owned a restaurant was very kind and generously served me a free steak. When I said goodbye, I challenged her to the need on the mission field. Shortly afterward, she sold her restaurant and became a missionary. A taxi driver also accepted my missionary challenge. Dozens of others, one by one, heard God's call to follow Him.

During this time, I was asked to speak at a town many miles away. After checking my wallet, I found only a few pennies. That evening Milly and I attended a prayer meeting. Rather fond of making fleeces (like Gideon in the Bible), Milly asked God to show her that He would provide for my trip. In the middle of the prayer meeting, she was tapped on the shoulder. "The Lord told me to give you this," a man said, as he placed a five-dollar bill in her hand. Needless to say, I went on the trip. I returned with more money than I had before!

During one of my trips, I was asked to take a candidate, Jon Cowpersmith, with me on the road. He was a brilliant student who came to us from a Pentecostal Bible school. He preached and taught better than any of us. Being single, he was housed in the boys' dorm. Each morning, he rose early and sang, prayed, and talked in tongues. During the day, he peppered every conversation with "hallelujah" and "praise God." At the end of his prescribed year of training, the concerned camp director refused to release him to the mission field.

"You are fanatical, Jon. You must stay in training for another year. Hopefully, you will become more balanced."

During that year, there was a devastating forest fire, and every able-bodied person was called upon to extinguish the fire. As a group, we strenuously labored all night. Jon not only worked along with us, but he also preached and worshipped God all through that difficult assignment. His enthusiasm kept all of our spirits up. The forestry department told us that if we had not participated, our camp would likely have been destroyed.

At the end of Jon's second year, his zealous behavior had not changed. The camp director came to me with a worried frown. "Well, uhm, we can't keep Jon here forever, so, uhm, let's uhm . . . Ted, I want to send him out with you on one of your trips across the country. By the time you're through, let's say you're gone a month or two, your balanced religious behavior will have rubbed off on him. Then perhaps we can send him into the field."

The morning we left, Jon sat in the car to read his Bible long before I was ready. As soon as we got out of the camp gate he said, "Listen to this, Brother Ware. Oh, praise the Lord, praise God, this is wonderful!" And he proceeded to read the first part of Psalm 63. "O God, Thou art my God; early will I seek Thee; my soul thirsteth for Thee, my flesh longeth for Thee in a dry and thirsty land, where no water is; To see Thy power and Thy glory, so as I have seen Thee in the sanctuary. Because Thy lovingkindness is better than life, my lips shall praise Thee. Thus will I bless Thee while I live: I will lift up my hands in Thy name".

At this, he raised his thin arms up, closed his eyes and sang a chorus, parts of it in something other than English, and we hadn't reached the bottom of the main road yet! I thought, *Oh, no. This is going to be some trip, this is.*

I drove, and he sang, read the Bible, prayed, and talked in tongues. This went on for a couple of months. Everywhere we went, he knew somebody. When we drove to the prairie, Jon said, "Now, Brother Ware, there's a couple of sisters that live just thirty miles from here. They've got a little church, and I know they'd be glad to see us. Why don't we stop and see them?"

Well, it was part of my job to promote the mission, so I said, "Well, yeah, sure, let's do that."

As time passed, I came to some startling conclusions. I realized for the first time, that there are two kinds of Christians: 1) Christians like me and my affiliation, who looked absolutely serious while the call for missionaries was shared with them. They were appreciative, unmoved and unexcited. When the offering plate was passed, we received a token response. That offering was our only financial support for our mission. On the other hand, 2) Christians like Jon and his affiliation, sat bright-eyed, enthusiastic, responsive, and they were givers! They always gave us a generous offering. The longer I observed these Christians, the more I was drawn to these "full gospel" Christians. They seemed to have life and vitality in everything that they did. I was most impressed with their singing and testimonies. They told of miraculous healings and answers to prayers.

During our meetings, I observed one old couple hugging each other and crying for joy. "My wife was given up by the doctors. She had cancer all through her body. I took her on a stretcher to a William Branham meeting. We got there late and sat in the back of the congregation. To our surprise, this minister called my wife by name, told her where we lived, and announced that God healed her of cancer. Sure enough, she bounced off of the cot and hasn't been ill since. The doctor can't find a trace of the cancer."

That night as I lay in the comfort of a bed in one of Jon's friend's home, I could not sleep. Jon was in the other single bed in the room. I whispered, "Are you awake?"

"Yes, I am."

"Tell me more, Jon."

"Well, Acts 2:38 and 39 says the promise is unto you, and to your children, and to all that are afar off, even as many as the Lord our God shall call. Healing and the baptism of the Holy Ghost go hand in hand. God said they were for us, and there's no place in the Bible where He retracted the promise."

"That little couple sure is grateful to the Lord for her healing, aren't they?"

"Anyone can believe for healing. It doesn't take a special minister." Jon told me many stories of his family and people he knew. Some had been healed in special meetings, others by simple prayer.

After Jon fell asleep, I thought about myself. I couldn't preach or speak like these people. They had more to say about God than I did, and I was a full-time Christian worker. I decided that it had something to do with this "baptism" that they talked about. Of course, I believed I received the Spirit when I was born again, but there must be some further experience that I was missing.

On our way back to the camp, two and a half months later, I was relaxed and delighted to be headed back to Milly and my children. Part of the journey took us around Lake Okanagan, which is about seventy miles long. The dirt road around it was narrow and full of curves. As I listened to Jon praise God, I was overcome by a wonderful, sweet feeling. I just felt good inside, so I said to Jon, "Jon, I think I'm getting blessed!"

Jon looked at me, and said, "Well, glory! Hallelujah!"

I responded, "Yes. Glory. Hallelujah."

To which he said, "Bless the Lord!"

"Yes. Bless the Lord," I replied. The pleasant feeling grew until I was filled with such joy that I was no longer aware of the road and started to praise God! There were no speed signs, and the car flew faster and faster around each curve. We came to a one-street town, slowed down, and decorously drove through it. As soon as we got to the other side, off we went again!

John began to speak in tongues, and lo, and behold, so did I! I had this marvelous experience of elation and anointing that I'd never had before. My heart filled to overflowing with love and concern for others.

When we got to Lake Kilowna, we stopped to drive on a ferry. I got out of the car and walked over to a group of Indians. I began to preach and witness to them. They probably thought I was crazy, but I couldn't resist sharing the joy I felt inside. We then drove on the ferry, crossed to the other side, and proceeded the last thirty miles to the camp.

When we pulled in about dusk, I jumped out of the car and rushed to Milly. "Darling, you won't believe what's happened!"

"What's happened?"

"I've been baptized in the Spirit!"

"That's wonderful! Praise the Lord!" she said excitedly. "And you're scheduled to speak to the students tomorrow morning!"

The following day, I gave a report of our trip and ended with my experience in the car. The leaders went from being quite happy, to being quite somber.

Following the meeting, the camp leader called me in to his office. "Now Ted," he used my preferred name, "we sent you to influence Jon, not for him to influence you."

"Yes, I remember. I did not ask for this experience other than praying to get nearer to God. I'm sorry that it upsets you, but I cannot disclaim something that has had such an effect on me."

"If you continue with it, you will be on your own."

"Let it not be said when we stand before God, that I did not trust Him on my own." I felt a peace that passed any understanding I'd ever had.

For the Sake of a Soul, 1954-1957

"**B**rother Ware, we do not agree with your fanatical experience. We had enough of Jon Cowpersmith and his speaking in tongues, and for sure, we will not put up with two of you! You are not to teach or lead in the mission, unless you renounce it. You have two weeks in which to make up your mind."

As Ted stood before the camp leaders, his heart cried out with his New Testament brothers, "We cannot but speak the things which we have seen and heard" (Acts 4:20).

After many tears, with saddened hearts, Ted and I agreed that we had no choice but to leave our camp family. "I'm going to miss them. No matter where God leads us, I want His blessings to be theirs also," Eddie said as we drove away.

"Why is it that we aren't bitter or angry, Eddie?" I asked.

"Because our experience was from God, and it makes us react as He would."

"Where is our home now, Daddy?" Clive asked as he saw the woodlands go by.

Nobody spoke for a few minutes. How do you tell your children that, "Foxes have holes, and birds have nests, but we have no place to lay our heads"(Matthew 8:20)?

"Our car is home now, because we are together in it," Eddie said. This seemed to satisfy Clive.

"Why did you give away your bed, Mummy?" Kevin asked.

We had carried our mattress from our home to the boot camp. I had given away my set of china dishes in order to focus on being missionaries. Now as we packed, I realized that if we planned to venture forth by faith with the Lord, we couldn't burden ourselves with all of the "comfort trappings" of the world. The mattress must stay.

"It wouldn't fit in the car," I answered Kevin.

We first drove to Vancouver where Eddie wanted to check on some financial opportunities. We knew that we had no money left in England. We had about ten dollars in our pocket, and we owned an old car. However, from the sale of our dream house, we were still owed $1500, to be paid to us in installments over many years. We drove to the house and asked the present owner, "What are the possibilities of your paying your debt to us early?"

The man replied, "Come back tomorrow, and I'll let you know."

So the next day we returned. "I'm going to make one offer," he said. "If you accept it, fine. If you don't, then the agreement will have to stay as it is."

So Eddie asked, "What's the offer?"

"One thousand dollars in cash."

"Done," Eddie said, and accepted the cash.

Later that night, I asked my husband as we snuggled together in a tiny bed in a friend's house, our children stacked like little sardines around us, "How did you feel in front of the house? Did you wish that it was ours again?"

"Milly, absolutely not. I'm more certain now than ever that one soul is worth a whole world of houses. If God will just bless us with souls, it will be worth it all. How about you? Do you miss your bed?"

"Yes, I miss it a little. But I wouldn't trade the peace I have in my heart for every bed in Canada! Eddie, where do we start to look for that soul or souls?"

"Well, with this house money, I think we should get a rugged, durable vehicle. Get rid of everything that doesn't fit in it and head out. The only destination that comes to my mind is British Guiana. There's a verse that says, 'I being in the way, the Lord led me.' So I think we should get 'in the way' and expect him to lead us!"

The next day we went to a vehicle dealer and looked at new Land Rover jeeps. Our $1000 was $200 short of their selling price. Eddie and I sat down on a bench in the show room and discussed how we could make payments on the $200 balance that we needed. At that moment, I looked up and saw an old Christian friend, Bob Lowe, walk into the building. He saw us and came over.

"It's so good to see you! Whatcha doin' here?"

"Well, buying a jeep, as a matter of fact, to take to the field with us," Eddie said.

"Oh, really? Well, I'd like to have a hand in that! Here." And without further ado, he made out a check for two hundred dollars.

The God we serve is so big that He can get small enough to know the number of hairs on our heads and the exact amounts of money it takes to buy a jeep. We bought the Land Rover outright that day; then we packed our worldly goods into it.

"I just added up what we have, Milly. Each other, five children, a new jeep, and fifty dollars."

Before we left boot camp, we received a letter from Eddie's family, who had all migrated to Canada. "Mother is in poor health. She has tuberculosis, and her kidneys are failing."

We traveled to Edmonton to see her. All of our children were allowed into her bedroom. Her eyes got big, "Look, Joe!" she said to Eddie's father. "All five of them are beautiful and healthy. Look at them, Joe!"

Apparently, she'd fretted that our children were malnourished and ill. She marveled at their height, strength, and robust health. "Isn't this a beautiful baby, Joe!" she said happily patting Paul's fair head.

Our hearts were heavy when it was time to go. As we drove away, Eddie said, "Mother pressed a $20 bill into my hand as we left and told me that it was for our children. Wasn't that kind? I wish that we could have stayed to help her."

"Yes," I replied, "I wish that we could have done more, but at least she knows that her grandchildren are fine. I talked to the doctor, and he told me that he did not know how long she has to live, and we have too many children to stay in their home with her so ill." Eddie agreed.

We traveled on to Calgary, where we knew a minister, Vic Graham, a friend of Jon Cowpersmith. We were welcomed and asked to sing a duet at an afternoon service. We sang *Speak, My Lord*, a song based on Isaiah chapter six: verse 8: "Also I heard the voice of the Lord, saying, whom shall I send, and who will go for us? Then said I, Here am I; send me."

As we concluded, the minister came behind us and prophesied a message from the Lord: "My children, I am with you. You have done what I wanted you to do. Go forward. I will lead you."

I felt a blanket of peace envelope me, and I thought, *No matter what happens, if God is leading us, we'll be all right.*

Encouraged, and with an additional $50 love offering from the church, we left Canada and headed south into America. Eddie had heard of a missionary convention going on in King's Gardens, Seattle, Washington, so we stopped there. One of the leaders came to Eddie and said, "Brother Ware, you are going to be our speaker."

Stunned, Eddie said, "I can't do that!"

"Oh, yes, you shall. The brother that we expected cannot get here, and the Lord has told us that you are to speak."

So Eddie spoke. I felt the anointing of God as he fervently shared what was in his heart. People responded and admitted that they had been moved in a wonderful way. Many unbelievers became Christians, and some that were not living for God, rededicated their lives to Him.

We received a telegram at this time that said. "Mother died. Left you this message: John 14." We knew the passage, but looked it up again:

Let not your heart be troubled: ye believe in God, believe also in me. In my Father's house are many mansions: if it were not so I would have told you. I go to prepare a place for you. And if I go and prepare a place for you, I will come again and receive you unto myself; that where I am there ye may be also. And whither I go ye know, and the way ye know. Thomas saith unto Him, Lord, we know not whither thou goest; and how can we know the way? Jesus saith unto him, I am the way, the truth, and the life: no man cometh unto the Father but by me.

We read to the end of the chapter and were comforted by the glorious truth of the Word of God. From her message, we believed that she supported our commitment, and that soon, after our tour of duty on this earth ended, we would see her in Heaven. She would be free from pain and sorrow, and we would never be separated again.

We could not attend the funeral but continued with the meetings.

Before the convention was over, Eddie had spoken at many Seattle high schools and prisons. We left Seattle with happy hearts, a full gas tank, and fifty dollars, plus many new friends, who said they would write to us if we kept in contact with them. One kind woman gave us a packed lunch as we pulled away from the convention grounds.

We went down the coast toward Portland, Oregon. As we chatted in the car, there was a loud pop, and the car swerved. "It's a flat tire," Eddie sighed and pulled the Land Rover to the shoulder.

"Milly, I'll put on the spare, then we'll pull into the next gas station to see what can be done."

At a gas station, I unpacked the lunch we had been given to feed the children. Tucked in the top of the neat basket was a five dollar bill. Just then, Eddie returned to the jeep, and said. "The problem can be taken care of for five dollars." I handed him God's answer. Isaiah 65: 24: "Before they call, I will answer; and while they are yet speaking will I hear."

We arrived in Portland and visited a Bible school. Then we continued south on Highway 101. Along that scenic coastal drive, Eddie affirmed, "Darling, isn't it wonderful!

Each time I check our assets, we still have fifty dollars! We were out of money, and then that church gave us an offering! God says that He will supply our needs, and thus far, He has. British Guiana, here we come!"

We researched ways to get to Guiana and found three: drive all the way down through Central America; take a boat from Louisiana across the gulf of Mexico; drive to the tip of Florida and take a boat across from there.

"Which way do you think that we should take?" I asked.

"Well, I think we'll just see which opens up to us." Eddie replied.

We stopped in Sacramento, California, at a Pentecostal church and found the lively congregation considerably different from any that we had met before. In one service, someone prophesied to Eddie, "You are surrounded by snakes and being attacked from all sides, but do not fear, it is going to be all right."

"How are we supposed to interpret that?" I asked Eddie after we left the church. I was really concerned about the snakes.

"I'm not sure, but at least the prophecy said that it would end up all right, whatever it means."

We asked travel agents and others about traveling through Mexico into South America. "There are no roads through southern Mexico, only a railroad, and it doesn't always work." We did not know Spanish, so we decided to take a boat. It sounded faster and less dangerous.

"What's the matter?" I asked Eddie, as he appeared withdrawn.

"I keep thinking that the Lord wants us to go to a leprosy colony, and I can't stand the idea."

"Oh, I see. Hmmmm. Well, He'll give us grace sufficient, I'm sure."

"I'll go anywhere else, Milly. Just not to a leprosy colony," he declared and was miserable for days.

He woke me early one morning, and I could tell that his gloom had lifted. "It's all right, Milly. I told the Lord that it was okay, that I'd go to a leprosy colony. And do you know what He answered?"

Fully awake, I answered, "No, Eddie, what?"

"That He didn't really want me to go to a leprosy colony; He just wanted me willing to go!" I rejoiced with him.

Since we had many miles to travel, Eddie built a little tent trailer for us to sleep in. We left California with more new friends, a jeep with a trailer, fifty dollars, and a church to contact. We were told that a church in Dallas, Texas, wanted us to stop and see them on our way through.

When we arrived in Dallas, the minister was delighted. "You're just the ones I need! I have a faith home here, and my nurse has been on duty for a month with no time off. Would you give her a vacation? I will pay you well for your work."

This seemed like a need that we should fill, so I went to work in the home and Eddie cared for the children.

The home was overcrowded with people, all believing that they would get healed. They sang songs and quoted Scripture at four and five o'clock each morning. This was admirable, but I was concerned that I did not witness any miracles. Some people had been there for a long time. Another concern that I had was the administration's attitude about money. The sick people paid to live in the building, but the money was not used for the welfare of the patients. On one occasion the minister asked the congregation to give our family a love offering. He kept all that was given but gave us ten dollars!

After two weeks at the faith home, the nurse returned. As we said goodbye, a blind old man gave Ted fifty cents, and a child gave him a penny. The ten dollars had gone earlier for food and gas, so we left with exactly fifty-one cents.

Our next stop was Houston, Texas, at a faith mission that had been recommended to us. This minister said, "Oh, It's good to see you! There's an apartment above the church that you're welcome to stay in. The freezer's full of food; just go up there and enjoy the weekend."

The next morning was Sunday, so our family attended church. A wonderful communion service was served around long tables. It was a sacred, beautiful experience.

Later that day, we were invited by the pastor: "We're having another meeting this afternoon, if you want to come down to it." We took the children and sat on the front seat. Following the service, people started to dance in worship to the Lord in the front of the church. The dancing was appropriate but totally strange to us.

A man came up to me and reached for Paul, who was two years old, and whispered, "I'll look after your children so you can dance."

I said, "No, no, no, thank you."

Three times people came up and offered to watch our children so we could dance. The last person said, "The Lord has told me to look after your children." So we left the children and joined the dancers.

I stood alone, then closed my eyes and moved slowly around, worshipping the Lord, oblivious to who or what was around. Minutes later, when I opened my eyes, I tugged on Eddie's arm. We were the only two up front! Everyone else was seated.

The minister stood and announced, "The Lord has separated this couple for us to give them a love offering. Now, I know we don't know them, but this is the Lord, and I want you to come up and bless them."

He turned to Eddie and said, "Open your Bible, brother." Eddie opened his Bible, and people came up and piled his Bible high with money. There was money everywhere.

Almost speechless after witnessing this miracle, Eddie said to the minister, "You know, all of my life I've wondered what it would be like to run around a church, and I feel like running. Would it be all right if I ran around the room?"

"Yes, do it."

So Ted ran around the church, and what do you think happened? The fifty-cent piece he was given earlier in the other church fell out of his pocket.

He stooped to retrieve it, and the Lord spoke to him, "I am no man's debtor. You were a blessing, now I'm blessing you. My Word says 'Give and it shall be given unto you, good measure, pressed down and running over'" (Luke 6:38).

That night there was yet another service. The minister's sermon title was "And the iron did swim," taken from 2 Kings 6:6. This Scripture portion describes how Elijah spoke, and an ax floated! I thought, *We need our jeep to float all the way to South America!*

At the end of the service, the minister said, "If you have anything in your hearts against anybody, stand up in your seat. Imagine you've got those bad feelings and thoughts in your hand, then throw them, and never think of them again."

Everybody got up and started to throw the imaginary things into God's Sea of Forgetfulness. I thought of a few things from the past, so started to throw along with everyone else. I went all the way back to my childhood. I went through my nursing experience and into Canada, forgiving as memories of unkindness came to my memory. I threw some things from the boot camp experience and days in Texas into God's Forgetfulness Sea. I even forgave myself and threw in some of my own faults and sins!

That night as Eddie and I went to bed I said, "I'm sure glad that God led us here. I feel clean and refreshed."

"Yes, it has been wonderful. A man came to me after church and wanted my car keys. I trusted him with them, and he returned our car full of gas. Also, the offering from the church congregation was fifty dollars!"

From Houston, Texas, we headed for New Orleans, Louisiana, where we heard there was a shipping company which had freighters that traveled back and forth to South America. After Eddie located the company, he came out of their office looking depressed.

"What did they say?" Clive asked.

"They said that it would cost $1,500 to get us and the jeep to South America." He stepped back into the jeep and started the engine.

"So what shall we do, dear?" I asked.

"There are other ports and shipping companies along the coast. At the end of Florida there have to be ways to get to South America; we'll just keep on traveling until we get to the end."

Our next stop was Mobile, Alabama. Ted parked the jeep and went into a store for some groceries while I sat in the car with the children. A stranger came up to my window and asked about our vehicle and where we were going. "The Lord has told me to take you home."

Shocked, I said, "Oh, really!"

"I'm serious," he insisted. "The Lord has told me to take your family home. I am a minister, and I'll be very pleased when your husband comes out, if you'll follow me home."

When Ted appeared, he met the minister and agreed to follow.

The pastor opened his church to us for meetings every night. Also, we were invited out to many homes where we were served fried chicken for breakfast, lunch, and supper! We'd never had so much fried chicken in our lives.

As we left Mobile, Ted informed us, "I just made a count: I've got my wonderful wife, five children, the jeep, and fifty dollars!"

In Florida, we stopped in Lakeland to visit the parents of some dear friends we had met in the California boot camp. They welcomed us as family. Before we left, they insisted that they would administer all our missionary correspondence. They maintained a current file of all interested persons in our missionary effort and printed and mailed our newsletters to those on that list.

While we were staying there, the children spent many happy hours riding horses and playing in the creek in the backyard. One afternoon I overheard our children in a heated discussion. Clive argued, "His name is Eddie."

"No, it isn't; it's 'Ted,'" Heather announced emphatically.

"His name is Edward Philip Ware, and sometimes people call him those other names," Kevin said.

"I know his real name," our toddler, Joy, said. "It's 'Daddy'."

As I listened, I realized that I had contributed to their confusion. I decided to call Eddie "Ted" in the future, to eliminate some of their confusion.

From Lakeland we traveled south to the tip of the mainland of America, the Florida Keys. When we arrived in Key

West, we were told at the dock that the cost to travel to South America was over $1,000.

Distressed by this "impossible" obstacle, Ted drove us to a beach, where I prepared a picnic. Since we did not have the needed $1,000, Ted went for a walk to pray for guidance. As I prepared the sandwiches and fed the children, I watched him wade into the water. Next he raised his arms into the air. Half an hour later he came back to the picnic table radiant.

Joyfully, he shared what the Lord had revealed to him. "I know what we're supposed to do!"

"Wonderful! What?" I asked.

"Well, I walked to the water's edge and felt that the Lord wanted me to take my shoes off, so I did. Then I waded into the water. I told the Lord that we had done all that we knew to do; that unless He supplied the funds, we couldn't go anywhere. Then I felt that He said, 'Are you done talking?' So I said, 'Yes.' Then He told me that He did not want us to go to British Guiana. That was the reason that He had not supplied funds. 'I want you to go to Cuba, which is but seventy miles from where you are standing.' So I believe that is what we need to do!"

I gulped, "All right, Eddie (I forgot about my resolve to call him Ted), then that's where we'll go."

We found an inexpensive fare, which included our jeep. Soon we were on a ferry to Cuba!

It was a beautiful, breezy day. Ted and I sat together on deck chairs and played with Joy and Paul. We all enjoyed watching the seagulls land on the deck and take crumbs of bread from passengers. Someone standing at the rail suddenly shouted, "Look at the flying fish!"

Kevin, Clive, and four-year old Heather, ran to the edge of the ferry to see the fish with wings!

Heather always carried her doll with her. Since our "jeep-home" was so small, Heather and all of the other children were permitted only one toy. Needless to say, Heather's doll was her constant companion. To give her doll a closer look at the flying fish, she hung it over the rail. A sudden gust of wind caught Heather off balance, pulling the doll from her tiny hand. It was a few seconds before she realized what had happened. Aghast, she watched over the rail as her beloved doll was engulfed by six-foot waves.

"My dolly's gone to be with Jesus!" she whispered. Tears ran down her cheeks.

A kind woman standing nearby heard her and asked, "Little girl, would you please take me to your parents?"

Heather brought her to where we were. "My name is Maxine Richardson. Your little girl says that 'her dolly went to be with Jesus'. Would you happen to be Christians?"

"Oh, yes indeed, we are," we said.

"I am also! I'm a missionary!"

"Well, we are, too!"

"Which denomination are you with?" she questioned.

"Well, no group, actually. We've had a Pentecostal experience, but we're not with any denomination."

"So where are you going in Cuba? Do you have a vehicle?" she queried. "Of course, you speak Spanish."

"We're going wherever God leads us, and yes, we have a vehicle, but we do not speak Spanish, yet."

The woman learned that we were missionaries to Cuba but surprisingly could not speak Spanish! She sat down on a vacant chair next to us and was silent for a few minutes.

"Maybe we can help each other. I need to get some barrels of supplies over to where I live at a Bible school. If you would carry me and my belongings, I could help you through customs, take you to where we work, then you would have time to decide what you should do next!"

We agreed. When we arrived in Cuba, Ted drove our vehicle off the ferry and strapped the woman's barrels onto the back of our jeep. I pushed things around inside, the children "doubled up," and somehow, we all managed to cram in and close the door.

We headed out of busy Havana, and a few hours later, arrived at the missionary woman's headquarters. The Bible school welcomed us. In the morning, we heard voices sing Christian songs in Spanish. How we wanted to join in with them in their beautiful language!

One day, as Ted was walking to the Bible school, he met an acquaintance from our original missionary training group, Buck Northrop.

"What are you doing here, Ted?" he asked.

They had a good visit recounting life since training camp. "I left the mission, too," he said, " and am working in a town farther east. We have a farm and a church there. Why don't you come and work with us? There are two houses on the property. My family lives in the front one. The back building will be ready for occupancy in a few weeks."

"Well, it sounds like a good place to begin," Ted said.

On the following day, we followed Buck to his church in Camajuani. Temporarily, we moved into a small apartment in town.

Everything was strange and new. Our neighbors lived so close that all day we heard their conversations but did not understand any of it. We heard their children crying, but we could not figure out why. Sometimes they laughed. For all we knew, they were laughing at us!

During this time of adjustment, Ted became extremely ill. I told our children, "Daddy has malaria. I am going to have to rely on you to help me, as I will have to nurse him."

We all gathered around Ted's bed and prayed. He smiled weakly at us. The next few weeks were very difficult. One minute Ted shivered, the next minute he drenched the bed with perspiration. Most of the time he was delirious. Buck Northrup came often and brought soup, fruit, and did whatever he could to help.

I became physically and emotionally exhausted. One day, as I hand-washed Ted's sheets for the second time that day, I wondered if we had made a mistake in coming to Cuba. Could this illness be considered the prophesied "snakes"? Up to this point I had found tarantulas in the apartment, but no snakes!

After three weeks, Ted was well enough to sit up; shortly after, he was able to walk. He was twenty pounds lighter when we moved out of the apartment in town to live in the country house behind Buck Northrup's home. Surrounding our new home there were banana trees and a big mango tree from which we hung a swing for the children.

A few months after we moved to the *finca* (farm), the Northrups returned to America. Since they suggested that we move into their larger house after they vacated it, we did. We decided our missionary work would continue in the country where there was no congregation. We noted that the town church had many missionaries and didn't need us. In the meantime, we could work on improving our Spanish speaking skills.

The first few times that Ted preached in Spanish, he drew good-humored laughs from the congregation. "The Epistle of Paul" came out as "The Pistol of Paul" (Epistola = Epistle, Pistola = pistol). Another time he greeted the people as "dear ladies and horses!" (Caballo = horse, caballero = gentlemen.) Everyone took these mistakes with good humor as his Spanish slowly improved.

As soon as we had an address, we wrote to our friends in England, America, and Canada, and the Jensens in Lakeland, about our new work in Cuba.

After a few months, donations came trickling in. The Canadian retired schoolteacher, whom I had thought looked like a witch when we first met her, sent us a five-dollar bill, carefully sewn onto a letter with black thread. A small church that we had visited on our way through California sent a check for ten dollars. We reported all the money that arrived in Cuba to the Jensens in Lakeland, who sent the donors our newsletter and receipts. Money came in slowly, only as we needed it, nothing more.

Careful with what we called "God's money" (which happened to be the only kind we had), we did not spend frivolously. Even though Heather wanted another doll to replace the one that had "gone to be with Jesus," Ted could not conscientiously buy one with "God's money." Happily, a few months later, we were sent funds that were designated specifically for the family, and Heather received a little doll.

On one occasion, our family was invited to eat at a Cuban family's home. The staple foods in Cuba are rice and black beans, with a slice of fried plantain banana on the side.

Children from left to right: Clive, Joy, Paul, Heather with her new doll, and Kevin.

Each of us was given a large plate of food. The children looked at us helplessly. The Bible tells us to eat such as is set before us, so we nodded to the children to try to clean their plates as we required at home. The precious "little missionaries" did a valiant job, and at last, they had clean plates. To our horror, no sooner had each of us finished, and our plates were refilled! Later, we learned the Cuban custom. A clean plate is a signal to the host that you want more food!

Over time we adjusted to the differences in cultures and to the strange new foods. We soon decided that the food was tasty and enjoyable!

Almost every night we held open-air meetings in villages in the country. The *campesinos* worked their fields during the day, and at night, were drawn to the vocal music and trumpet playing. They also found our Coleman lantern and battery-driven PA system fascinating. A native speaker was always on hand to speak. Ted saw himself as a catalyst missionary: to start the spiritual fire, then move on to spark more fires.

After the Northrups left for America, new missionaries replaced them. They did not agree with our goals, but adamantly asserted that things must be done their way. "Their way" did not include the *campesino* work. Ted and I then decided to continue our work independently.

We moved to a 200'x 600' property outside of a town called Tarafa, where a country, Cuban house was built for us. These simple houses are made entirely from the beautiful, sixty-foot tall Cuban royal palm tree. Protected by the government, special permission is required to cut them down to build a house. Ted watched in awe as our home was built. The trunk of the tree was split in half to make the walls. The dried branches became the roof, and the green fronds were used to tie the dry thatch in place. The bark from under the fronds was used to cover the crown of the roof, where the thatch met, to keep the rain out. The finishing touches were the cement floor, the hinged-board windows, and a simple wooden front door. A well with a bucket supplied the water, and there was an outhouse.

A railroad track crossed the main street in front of our house. Along with the train noises, there was the constant sound of car horns being used. Cubans used their horns to say hello and goodbye. Taxis, all big American cars with beefed-up horns, honked indiscriminately and continually.

After we settled into our new home, we sent Kevin and Clive to local Cuban schools. This arrangement did not work out very well, since they did not know Spanish, and I also worried that they would miss the basics in their education. The children became fluent in Spanish in six months.

During that time, I had decided to home school them by a correspondence course, to assure their basic education.

One day, Adelle came to our home. She said that she was a Christian, and asked if she could stay with us and learn English. She offered to help around the house and with the children. She was a godsend.

At first, Adelle cared for Heather, Joy, and Paul, while I taught Kevin and Clive. Our school day began at 8:00 A.M., with Bible reading and prayer. The subjects: mathematics, English language, and social studies, filled the rest of the morning. Unfortunately, the children had no art or sports training.

Visitors from America often requested to use our children as their interpreter, but I was adamant that each child's lesson be completed first. Clive did not enjoy schoolwork. He wanted to be outside with animals and bugs. In Cuba, there were many: rats, mice, frogs, scorpions, mosquitoes, *caballo del diablo* (devil's horse, which are flies with horrible stings), and centipedes. Also, our yard housed hundreds of tarantulas. Clive collected them in our metal bathtub. He tricked them from their holes by tapping lightly on the ground, which apparently sounded to the ugly creatures like rain. As the tarantula emerged, Clive the naturalist, prodded it onto the end of a long stick, then quickly transferred the stick with the tarantula end into the tub. A little tap and it fell in. Sometimes a spider fell off of the stick before it reached the tub. Then Clive scurried around it, until it reluctantly got back onto the stick. In a very short time, the bottom of the tub was covered with tarantulas crawling over each another.

One evening, Ted found all of his children in the backyard bent over the tub, admiring the amazing creatures. He asked Clive to dispose of them.

If at any time a visitor desired to see a tarantula, Clive knew how to quickly find one. Since he would first look in our thatch rafters, I wondered if he hadn't "disposed" of some of them there.

Cuba was also a land of frogs. One particular large, green, banana tree frog had elongated legs and fingers with suckers on each fingertip. These suckers were obviously designed by God, so that the frog could climb up the slick banana tree trunk. Ted loathed frogs, particularly if they appeared in our thatched ceiling. We never knew when one would appear right by our side, or in front of us, or on us.

One night it was very hot and humid. Over each bed was a mosquito net, but during this night, Ted removed our net to feel more airflow. Still unable to sleep because of the heat, he also took his pajama top off. He then lay in bed and tried to get some sleep. All of a sudden, I heard a yell to wake the dead! One of the huge frogs with the sucker type fingers had jumped onto Ted's bare chest! He grabbed the frog and threw it across the room, then continued to yell, "Clive! Clive! Come quick! Get this creature out of here!" Clive was pleased that he was the official amphibian remover!

In addition to their schoolwork, we taught them other skills. To teach the children responsibility, we allowed each of them to have their own animal. Clive owned a cockerel that he had raised from a little ball of fluff. It had grown big and strong and had beautiful, brightly-colored plumage. It lived in a tree beside the house and each morning woke us up with its crowing. We almost depended on it to wake us up. One morning, however, it did not crow. It had disappeared!

Clive became very sad. "Mum, where could my cockerel have gone? It never leaves the area around our house."

"Maybe a dog got it, Clive."

"No, I've seen it around dogs, and it always flies up into its tree!"

"Well, Clive, we can certainly pray and ask God to bring it back home for you."

"Yes, let's pray," Clive agreed. We prayed that the bird would come back, and after the prayer, Clive was sure that it would return.

A long week went by. Half way through the second week, Clive happened to be over at the neighbor's yard and found his cockerel, unquestionably his cockerel, in a pen. Cubans enjoyed cockfights, and because Clive's bird was so big and beautiful, the neighbor's teenager had taken it to train to cockfight. When Clive saw it, he told the boy's father, "That's my cockerel!"

The father said, "Really?" Then turned to his son, "Did you steal this boy's cockerel?"

"Oh, no, no!" the teenager assured his father.

"Undo the pen. If it's Clive's cockerel, it will know where it belongs," the wise adult said. The latch on the pen was undone, and the cockerel strutted across the field, through the hedge to its own tree, and cried, "cock-a doodle-do!" Apparently, God counts more than just sparrows!

We also had other animals. We used our horses for the Christian work, and sometimes we rode as a family along the dirt path by the railroad. As we rode out of town, the country opened up into fields, the tall royal palms swaying overhead. Oxen plowed the rows of tobacco and sugar cane. Thatch-roofed huts dotted the landscape where the farmers lived. Bordering the farmer's property, special sticks were hammered into the earth that took root and grew into beautiful tree fences. We often continued our ride outside of town to a river and swam in the cool water.

Occasionally our postman advised us that a parcel had arrived from America. Before we were able to take it from the post office, we were always required to pay high *aduana* (import taxes) on it. The contents were rarely worth the cost of the tax. An example is a parcel containing a skirt, with a burn the shape of an iron, and a roll of twelve-inch pieces of broken string wound together! That was the contents of one package!

I often thought that if I had the time, I could possibly make something out of these discards, but being busy with the work, there was never enough time! Also, I did not have a sewing machine.

One year, however, I hand-sewed Joy and Heather each a dress with some fabric that I bought locally. I took extra time to embroider flowers on the front. When the girls wore

A Cuban "Campesino" House

them they looked pretty. To my chagrin, the day that I washed them, they disintegrated. The fabric was rotten!

One time a parcel came from someone who sent us a real treat, a little jar of strawberry jam! How we stretched that *dulce* (sweet)! We allocated a small amount each week to each member of the family. One day, the strawberry "treasure" was on the table, when a Cuban worker came for lunch. We often invited native workers to eat with us. He plopped the entire month's ration of our treat onto his plate, as we, salivating, watched him devour it.

It was understandable that we were never overjoyed when we were notified of a parcel's arrival; so at another time, when we were told that a parcel awaited us, I groaned to Ted, "Oh, no." But this one was different. Some of the congregation we'd met in Alabama sent it, and obviously they had prayed over it. The post office also amazed us, because they did not require any *aduana* on it, even though it was a sizable box! Inside the box were two sets of brand new clothes for everyone in the family. Everything fit perfectly. A true gift from heaven.

Our missionary work began to flourish as native workers from Cuba's Bible colleges and other missionaries came to help. One night, Ted and I discussed the need for a bigger vehicle. "Our little jeep is not big enough to carry the workers, equipment, and the literature we need." We then purchased a larger jeep and traded in the smaller one.

We also upgraded our home to a large house in Santa Clara, a much bigger town. Since there was a front room to sort and store Christian literature, and rooms for guests to stay, we moved into it.

God also sent Kathy U'Ren from Washington state to help with the work. Adelle did not move with us to Santa Clara, so I was happy to have Kathy assist with the household and secretarial work. She also played the accordion. This was an asset in the country services. Len and Connie Hearn came from Canada with their daughter Marguerite and lived in a small house across the street.

Our missionary outreach kept us all so busy that we paid little attention to Cuban politics. The country farmers were too occupied eking out an existence to worry about who their nation's leaders were. Batista, the present president of the country, allowed religious freedom, which made it possible for us to distribute literature and hold meetings wherever there was interest.

In 1958, Fidel Castro started a major campaign to overthrow the Batista government. Using guerrilla tactics, he began in the eastern tip of the country. By the time he reached our central location, he had his system in place. Over short wave radio, he made regular broadcasts: "Revolt! Strike! Light fires in the streets! I bring to Cuba a wonderful new era of wealth and happiness!"

The populace ignored his demands so he broadcast another message: "You are now under a curfew. Anyone found out of their homes after ten o'clock at night will be shot."

At first, the people laughed, since this threat would hinder their customs. One practice that all of the youth enjoyed was on Saturday and Sunday nights, the boys walked around the town square in one direction, and the girls walked in the other. As they passed and eyed each other, friendships developed, and by the end of the evening, they all walked in one direction in pairs. This, and other nighttime activities, ceased after many people were shot.

Fidel's men literally burned many bridges. Their favorite tactic was to ambush buses on the one-lane bridges, empty them of people, and burn them. This accomplished two things. It destroyed the bus, and the bus's gasoline fueled the burning of the bridge. Over most of the rivers, there was an alternate route, so traffic was crippled, but not stopped.

In late 1958, a neighbor was taken from his home by Batista's soldiers. We never saw him again. Military vehicles often drove by full of men with guns. We were told about young men leaving town and joining up with Castro. Realizing that it was a dangerous time, we always prayed before engaging the engine on our vehicle to go anywhere.

Missionary Work in Cuba and the Ambush, 1958

Say not ye, There are yet four months, and then cometh harvest? Behold, I say unto you, Lift up your eyes, and look on the fields; for they are white already to harvest. And he that reapeth receiveth wages, and gathereth fruit unto life eternal: that both he that soweth and he that reapeth may rejoice together. And herein is that saying true, One soweth, and another reapeth. I sent you to reap that whereon ye bestowed no labour: other men laboured, and ye are entered into their labours. (John 4:35)

Before we arrived in Cuba, evangelist T.L. Osborne visited the island, with a mighty moving of the Holy Spirit. Thousands were saved, healed, and delivered from the power of evils that had blighted their lives. In the town of Camaguey, there had always been a small full gospel church of a few dozen people; after the revival, it was packed with over five hundred. The local government under Batista gave land for a new church building, right in the heart of that town. The people were called *los aleluyas* (the "hallelujah people"), since they constantly praised God, so the church building was named *"Templo de Aleluya"* (Temple of Hallelujah). The name, printed in twelve-foot letters across the front of the building, could be seen for miles. Due to this "sowing of the seed" by Brother Osborne, wherever we went in Cuba, crowds of people, hungry for God, came to listen. We found "reaping" quite easy.

Since our Spanish-speaking skills were weak, we used Christian films from Moody Bible Institute as tools to deliver God's simple message of salvation. One film that the country folk especially enjoyed showed a caterpillar turn into a butterfly, which beautifully represented how God, who created all nature, also had the ability and desire to change our lives. Another piece of equipment we used was a small public address system that contained a tape recorder connected to a loudspeaker that could broadcast as far as two miles. It operated from a hand-crank generator.

While in Cuba, we gave out tons of Christian literature and Bibles. On one trip into an isolated area, I was welcomed into the thatch-roofed home of a tiny old lady. To my surprise, she already knew Christ as Savior. *How could this be,* I wondered, *as there were no churches or other Christians for miles around her?*

"Forty years ago, a missionary came and left a tract with me. I sent for a Bible from the address on the back, and through reading it, I became a Christian."

I was thrilled at the power of the Word of God. Truly it would "not return void, but would accomplish that for which it was sent." (Isaiah 55:11)

In another remote area, we held an evangelistic meeting and left tracts, New Testaments, and copies of the Gospel of John. Six weeks later, we were able to return, and to our surprise, found Cubans holding their own service with the aid of the Bibles and literature we had left. This group became the strongest church in our field of service.

The World Home Bible League provided so much literature per our request that at one point, they sent a person down to check if the material was actually getting used. They found their Bible literature had a very short "shelf life."

We had twelve full-time workers whose sole job was to minister and to give out literature and New Testaments in *los campos* (the country areas). I had a vision that burned within me, to train native workers, who would then, not only spread God's good news to fellow Cubans, but to every Spanish-speaking country on the globe.

One worker, Bernardo Ocampo, was a five-foot-two giant for God. When we met him, he was already a Christian. He had been a prosperous businessman, owning his own store. Often he told his wife before they heard of Christ, "Truly I have everything: two fine children, a home, a good income, and real friends, thanks to Santa Barbara."

Ocampo kept images of Santa Barbara and other idols throughout his home. He reverently worshipped them each night as he lit a small oil lamp and placed fresh flowers as a gift before them.

Cuban religion was a mixture of Catholicism and voodoo. When Ocampo or his family got sick, he called on the voodoo man, who charged him, and then practiced his powers. Each day Ocampo's friends told him how lucky he was as they drank, smoked, and played cards together in his store.

One day, one of these friends told him, "A crazy foreigner is downtown preaching. You should go hear him. It's a scream the things that he says, and his Spanish is hilarious!"

The opportunity for entertainment was not to be missed. Ocampo decided to go with his friends and his wife with hers.

The men arrived late, but heard the missionary declare, "Only through the shed blood of Jesus Christ can a person find remission of sin. Salvation is only available to those who accept what Christ accomplished on the cross."

Ocampo prayed to saints, but was he "saved?" When the missionary said, "Anyone who wants to be saved and have their sins forgiven, raise your hand." Strangely, Ocampo felt an unseen presence urge him to raise his hand. What would his wife and friends think? They would certainly laugh at him. His hand went up.

The missionary then asked those who raised their hand to walk forward. When Ocampo shouldered his way through the crowd to the front and knelt down, he gasped in surprise as his wife came and knelt beside him. She slipped her hand into his.

Later that night, as he worshipped before the shrine of Santa Barbara, he could not put his heart into it. However, he feared that the saint would bring misery and evil into his life, if he did not pay her due respect.

The next day the missionary reassured him, "Don't fear. Tell God your problem."

At home, he knelt beside his bed with his wife and poured out his heart to God. He asked God, "*Por favor*, please show me what to do about all of my saints, especially Santa Barbara. I am afraid of what will happen if I don't worship her shrine."

As the words left his lips, he heard a sharp crack. Startled, he got up and looked around. In the living room, he found the oil lamp broken in many pieces, and flames were licking Santa Barbara's feet. A big fat bug was trapped in the bowl and exploded from the heat. That night, Ocampo, certain that God had answered his prayer, and his wife, took a hammer and broke all of their shrines. They stripped their walls clean of "sacred pictures," and threw them out their front door, a pile of trash for everyone to see. With joy and peace, they went to bed and slept soundly. He was delivered forever from the bondage of idol worship.

In the days that followed, Ocampo threw the store liquor and tobacco away and stopped the gambling. He began to study the Scriptures day and night and found other Christians to fellowship with.

Business dwindled and persecution began. All of his acquaintances left him. Many that owed his store money did not pay their debts. Only his faithful wife and children remained. All of this happened before we arrived in Cuba. When we heard his story, we rejoiced and encouraged him to share his testimony at our meetings. As he spoke, the crowds were riveted by his simple words.

Later, Ocampo sold his store and worked full time for God. He poured his heart out night after night, and hundreds of his countrymen were lead to the Lord.

Another full-time worker, Mundo, regularly took a horse out in the mornings, his saddlebags full of literature to distribute.

He returned one afternoon with an interesting account. "Brother Ware," he said, "one of the farmers I visited was not interested in what I had to say, so I left his house and found my horse sitting down outside. I did everything I knew to get it back on its feet. I said to it, 'Please, good horsey, please get up. This farmer does not want us on his property. Please take me to the next farm.'

"But no matter how much I begged and pulled on his reigns, he would not budge. Then I pushed and heaved at his backside, but he is so big, he did not move one inch. I said to the horse, 'If I have to leave you with this un-Christian farmer, you will deserve what treatment you get! This is very un-Christian behavior, horse!'

"You know, Brother Ware, this is one of our better horses. It's normally a very agreeable creature. So, next, I got a stick and poked him with it. He wouldn't budge.

"At last I went back into the farmhouse for help and found the farmer now ready to accept the Lord! I led him to the Lord. When I was done, I went outside, and the horse was standing on its feet, happy to leave. Isn't it wonderful? Brother Ware, even our horses work for God!"

Many of the young evangelist nationals were graduates from Cuban Bible schools but still shy in front of crowds. I encouraged them to speak in the meetings. They stammered, and stood on one leg, then the other, as they "tried their wings." Within a very short time, nearly all of them became fiery preachers of the gospel, able to perform joyous baptismal services and talk to large crowds.

Often poor people gathered at these services, men dressed in shirts that were a solid network of patches, and women in simple, homemade dresses. They eagerly listened to Scripture and the words of life from the workers.

"One soul saved is worth all of the comforts that we left behind," Milly sometimes had to remind me. Particularly, when a visitor from Canada said to me, "I keep my cows in a better place than this," as he walked around our house. His disdainful words hurt and depressed me.

One afternoon later, a soaking tropical downpour trapped me in the house. The thatch roof leaked, and mud formed six inches deep all around the house. In a gloomy mood, I looked around me. We had no comfortable furniture. Cracks in the board walls let in a chilly breeze. There was no running water, except the leaks, and no light, except for a temperamental lantern. The wooden windows made the house even darker when they were shut to keep the rain out. When I went outside to use the outhouse, I found the cement seat occupied by two green frogs.

Then my mind flashed back to the luxury of hot water, dry, comfortable rooms with carpet, furniture, and glass windows. I thought of apples, ice cream, coffee, and cars. To further dampen my spirits, I had just been told that one of the new Christians had been found stealing. "What is the use?" I groaned.

That evening I was due to take a group of workers to an open-air meeting, deep in the *campo*. I looked at my watch and saw that it was time to leave. I kissed Milly on her neck as she bent to tuck one of our children, who happened to have measles, into his makeshift bed, and to pray with him.

"Have a wonderful service, dear. I'll be praying for you," she told me.

I grunted my thanks and trudged outside to the jeep. Only a few workers showed up, and I was tempted to cancel the trip. "No," I thought, "there are dear ones who trust us with their offerings and prayers."

I pushed the starter button, and we began the bumpy trip, the windshield wiper working hard.

Three *senoritas* in the back began to sing, "*Mi corazon contento esta, porque Jesus ya me salvo*" (my heart is happy because Jesus saved me). I started to feel better.

At last we arrived at a small village, to find only a handful of people waiting to hear us. I pulled my trumpet out of its case and began to play as if for the king and queen of England. (I had noticed previously that if I played carelessly, the people sang without enthusiasm.) We had prayer, testimonies, and finally, the native speaker gave a message. At the conclusion, he offered an invitation for salvation.

An old lady raised her hand. The privilege of seeing her face light up as she accepted Christ's gift of salvation completely changed everything for me. I appreciated the old jeep as I packed up our equipment and my heart sang for joy over each bump in the trail. Hallelujah, a soul saved! Only one, but worth more than the wealth of the world.

That night, as I fell asleep next to my precious wife, I thought kindly of the old "cow barn" that we lived in: the lantern's glow seemed warm; rice and beans delicious; even measles and mud took on a new aspect. Tomorrow the sun would come out and dry the ground, and within a few days, the children would be well again. I thought of the *campesinos* that we ministered to. They had a lot less of this world's goods than we did. We could not balance all the inequality, but we could offer them all that we had: love, peace, joy, purpose, blessings innumerable, and heaven!

Juana, a vivacious little woman in her forties, had a testimony much like Ocampos's. Her home, too, was full of statues and religious pictures. Her entire family faithfully kissed them each morning before they started their day. The pictures became grotesque over time, as the constant touch of their lips wore huge holes in them.

One day, Juana heard God's message of love and forgiveness as we sang and testified in her village. She learned that the price for her sins was totally paid by our Lord Jesus Christ on Calvary. How she rejoiced! Following that meeting, she collected all of the religious artifacts in her home, took them outside, and burned them. Her neighbors asked her, "Juana! What are you doing?"

She responded, "God says in my Bible, 'Thou shalt have no other Gods before me.'" When we heard about it, we were thrilled that the Word of God spoke for Itself.

Jill (pronounced "Hill") was another convert. He lived next door to us, so we knew his life quite well. He was a traveling salesman. Each morning, he packed his horse with his merchandise: matches, candles, salt, and other staples, and headed off into the countryside to peddle his goods.

By nature, he was mean and sometimes violent. We watched as people crossed to the other side of the street when he came down the road. His home was the same as the thatched roof house that we lived in. His wife cooked inside on an open fire, as was the custom, and we often watched the smoke from it sleepily drift up through the thatch of their roof. Inside their home, they sat on boxes and ate at a box table.

Jill's daughters, Aurelia and Tita, regularly attended meetings in our home. They accepted Jesus as their Savior and begged their papa to come to the services. He would always refuse.

Then, to our surprise, one night he came. He sat on the side of the room, up front, and scowled throughout the service. At the end of the meeting, we gave an invitation for salvation. Jill stood up, looked around, then sat down. We were puzzled but prayed with him before he went home.

The next morning, early, there was a banging on our door. I got up to answer it.

"*Hola* (hello), Jill!" What can we do for you?" I asked sleepily.

"Well, you know those little books that you give out?"

"Yes."

"Have you got any?"

"Yes."

"Well, I want some," he requested and looked at me earnestly.

"Oh? What do you want some for?"

"Well, to give them out!" He sounded indignant.

I apologized and hurried to get him some literature. He gave the booklets out and told others about Jesus wherever he traveled. One of the first persons that he led to the Lord was his old father. Next was his wicked sister. The patriarch was so happy to see the changes in his family that he wanted to give something back to God. He generously offered the use of his home for services and for the work of God.

Jill banged on our door early another morning. "Brother Ware! Brother Ware! Come over and see what God has done for me!"

I went over and found actual furniture in his home!

"How did you get this, Jill?" I asked, pleased with the improvement.

"Yesterday, on my route, a man was on the trail with a cart load of furniture that he was taking to the market to sell. I asked him about buying the whole cart load. Since I

Cuban Pig Roast

no longer drink or smoke, and the price was low enough, I had enough money to buy all of it!" I rejoiced with him.

For a third time, early in the morning, I was awakened. "Come see! Come see! Oh, this is wonderful! God is so good to me!" Jill shared enthusiastically. I rushed behind him. He took me to his hog pen. There to my amazement lay a sow with six piglets!

"My sow has never had more than two piglets. Never. And with six we can eat for many days!" Again, I went home rejoicing over his blessings.

A month or so went by then he rattled our front door once again. "*Hermano* (Brother) Ware, *Hermano* Ware! *Ven a ver!* (Come see!) *Ven a ver!*" So I scurried over.

There in his yard stood a sickly cow. "Oh, Brother Ware, never in my life did I dream that I would own a cow. Never. It is marvelous! I was on the trail and a man passed me with it. He was selling it for a very low price, so I bought it!"

His vices had kept him bound in poverty for so long that now that he was released, he was thrilled with his new life and its many opportunities.

I thought to myself as I walked home, *The cow looks sick. That's why he was able to buy it so cheaply. It's probably on its last legs. But Jill sure looks happy, so I'll just rejoice with him.*

I enjoyed my early morning rest for a few months more when again I thought that the door would not hold up to the physical assault, "*Hermano* Ware! *Hermano* Ware! *Es maravilloso!* (It is marvelous!) *Ven a ver!*" Of course, I ran behind him to his home.

He had constructed a shelter for his cow. He pointed for me to look over the shelter wall. There on the floor of the pen lay a beautiful calf beside its contented mother. Jill excitedly repeated over and over, "Can you believe it, Brother Ware? Now I have two cows!" We both stood at the wall and gazed in awe at the new life. We praised God for His care, love, and provision!

Another great blessing was the salvation of Challo. He was the hopeless town drunk in a village next to us. His niece, Anita, was a Christian, and constantly loved and prayed for him. She had pleaded with him innumerable times to become a Christian, but he had always rejected her requests.

One night, while she was in a meeting, she had a foreboding fear for her uncle. I watched as she slipped out of the service. She later told me that she had run to where he lived and opened the door. There she found him on the floor, drunk as always, with a big kitchen knife raised to cut his wrists.

"Oh, Uncle! Don't do that! Uncle dear, please don't do that! Come with me to church, Uncle. Don't hurt yourself, please!"

Somehow, she was able to get him to the meeting. She returned to her seat, but her uncle would not sit down. He drunkenly staggered up to the pulpit where Giraldo, another of the workers, was quietly preaching. Everyone in the congregation was frightened and jumped up onto the bench seats, talked excitedly, and, in fear, watched the intoxicated man as he fumbled around. I asked another worker to help him out of the building, which he did, and everyone settled back down. Giraldo spoke, unfazed, throughout the uproar. He had a message, and he was going to finish it.

I started to relax again, when *bang*! The back door flew open, and the drunkard stumbled in. Chaos and excitement disturbed the meeting, and again I asked that he be removed.

A third time, *bang*! The determined man went from bench to bench, all the way to the front, where Giraldo continued to preach. At this point, I decided that the meeting was ruined, so I picked up my things to leave. When I glanced up at the pulpit, the drunkard stood not twelve inches from Giraldo's face. In awe at the speaker's perseverance, I then watched the intoxicated man fall to his knees. He raised his hands and asked God to forgive him.

Thrilled, we all gathered around him and prayed.

The next day he told his niece, "I am a new man! Everything is new! This sandwich that I am eating tastes wonderful! The sky is beautiful! The sunshine feels good!"

She rejoiced with him and thanked God continually for his salvation. He started to help with church services and became a blessing to many.

In the summer of 1958, we drove to the Oriente province, and to our amazement, were stopped twelve times by soldiers. They were looking for revolutionaries, who usually dressed in green fatigues and had long hair, often worn in a ponytail.

As we talked with the soldiers, we were able to convince them that we were not interested in politics, and they often accepted our tracts and New Testaments.

As the revolution escalated, however, there were times we were stopped at the point of a gun. When either the revolutionaries or the Cuban soldiers discovered who we were and what our ministry was, they always let us go. Both Fidel Castro and Batista's men gave us freedom to continue to minister, since we were apolitical. We desired only to reach out to people at a time when they needed it. We proceeded without fear to: "Take the Word, preach the Word, and leave the Word."

During that time, I took a quick trip to Canada to talk to individuals and churches about the needs in Cuba, which were more literature and workers. The trip was successful, as I was promised that they would send both.

One young woman, Kathy U'ren, from Washington state said that she would give a year of her life to help in any way that was needed. She played the accordion well and had excellent secretarial skills. We were thrilled when she arrived and put also "her hand to the plow." (Luke 9:62)

Another wonderful family addition was Len and Connie Hearn, and their daughter, Marguerite. Brother Len was enthusiastic and talented in writing and photography. His wife was a nurse, and his pretty daughter was a typical teenager, not altogether thrilled to be in Cuba.

On Sunday, November 16, 1958, we were invited to conduct an evening evangelistic service in a small village called Viana. After lunch that afternoon, Milly said, "Ted, I don't feel good about going out tonight. Maybe we shouldn't go. Even Kathy isn't enthusiastic."

"Well, I don't feel really peaceful about it either, but we're expected, and many people will be disappointed if we don't."

"Who of us is going?" she asked.

"There are the Hearns, and their daughter, Marguerite, Kathy U'Ren, you and I, and the children. That's eleven. It's a good thing we have the bigger jeep, isn't it!" I said. We had just bought a larger Land Rover. She smiled, and proceeded to the kitchen to clean the dishes.

That evening, before leaving for Viana, we bowed our heads and prayed. "Lord, we thank you for all of your provision and blessings. We thank you that we can go out. In First Corinthians 1:21 it says it 'pleased God by the foolishness of preaching to save them that believe.' We pray that through our small, foolish efforts, you will save souls."

We arrived at the hall in the little town of Viana, set up the musical instruments, and proceeded with the service. The benches that had no backs were full. After the service, several people came forward for prayer. We felt we had ministered God's message to the congregation. As we packed our equipment to return home, we were told that refreshments had been made to honor our visit. We all preferred to leave, but to be polite, we stayed until we had eaten a little. It was dark when we climbed into our Rover.

On the twisting, narrow road home, we talked about Christ's return. I drove and Milly sat next to me. Our toddler, Paul, and Kathy U'Ren, were also in the front seat. In the back half-seat sat Brother and Sister Hearn and Marguerite, their daughter. Sister Hearn picked up and held our six-year-old Joy, who had fallen asleep on the floor. On the back bench-seats sat our other children, Heather, Clive, and Kevin.

Brother Hearn commented, "I think that the second coming of the Lord is the vital message for the hour, both for the comfort of the saints, and the warning of judgment to those who refuse God."

Milly added, "When I was a child, my father opened the drapes to the morning light with, 'I wonder if it's going to be today?' He lived for Christ's second coming, didn't he, Ted?"

"He sure did. He often said, 'He's coming in the clouds, and every eye shall see Him. We'll all be caught up together to meet Him in the air.' That sure is a wonderful promise."

We had passed through the village of Cienfuentes, when suddenly, there was a loud bang.

Kevin shouted, "Dad, we've got a flat!" I knew we did not have a flat tire; it was the bark of a gun.

I knew we were being attacked! I needed to get the dome light on. Now, this new Land Rover jeep had been quite satisfactory to me in all details, except that the dome light switch was positioned over on the passenger's side of the dashboard. This made it a nuisance to get to. As I leaned in front of Milly, I heard the roar of many guns.

Fidel Castro's young rebels were preparing to burn the bridge that we approached, and they thought that we were Batista's men, who had come to arrest them. The first shot had been the lookout's warning shot to his comrades. A large .45 caliber bullet pierced the side door of the vehicle, in the same spot Joy had lain before Sister Hearn picked her up. The bullet that missed Joy went into Marguerite's right heel, and then continued into her left heel.

The second barrage was from the machine guns of twenty-four scared rebels, not more than fifty feet away from us. They shot at us from the dark embankment, their guns aimed upwards. My head was in front of Milly as I attempted to turn the interior light on. I felt a wallop, like a blow from a hammer, to my head. One of my eyes switched off. I remembered hearing that Englishmen are "hard-headed." Since that night I have not been able to live that down. My head stopped four bullets. Three lodged in my skull, but did not penetrate the brain. Another bullet pierced my eyebrow, traveled through the back of my eye, slicing the optic nerve, then lodged in my jaw.

The truth that God is the mighty God of miracles became abundantly clear to me that night. If I had not been bending over in front of Milly, four machine gun bullets would have ripped through her chest. With four bullets in my head, I was able to turn the dome light on and also stop the jeep. There was no panic. God gave us his peace.

The soldiers emerged from the shrubs; the ends of their guns still smoking. One of the rebel leaders leaned his head through the door. "What are you doing here? We thought you were the enemy."

"We are missionaries, returning from a meeting in the country. We have no interest in politics."

As he turned from my window, I realized that there was blood everywhere. I was handed a pillow, which I held over my face to stop the flow of blood. Somebody put Kathy's shawl around my shoulders. I didn't know that I'd been hit with four bullets, but I knew I was seriously hurt. Len Hearn stepped out of the jeep and began handing out tracts and witnessing to the rebels!

The young leader of the group, his beret down over his forehead, came to my window. I asked him, "Do you have a doctor?"

"No."

"Well, have you got another vehicle that we could use?"

"No, we haven't."

"How far is it to the nearest doctor?"

"Eight kilometers back, the way that you came."

Here we were, Marguerite and I seriously wounded, one light of our vehicle shot out, the windshield shot out, the

BULLET-RIDDLED jeep windshield behind which missionary Edward Ware, his wife, five children and others were sitting when a burst of sub-machine gun fire was loosed by Fidel Castro's rebels in Cuba (shown here with Len Hearn behind the wheel).

radiator with bullet holes in it, and we had eight kilometers of night driving ahead. How were we going to get back? Len handed out what New Testaments we had left from the meeting and stepped back into the Rover.

We had a prayer meeting for a few minutes, thanked God for His mercy that we were all still alive, and asked Him to heal Marguerite and me.

Brother Hearn suggested, "Brother Ware, let me see if I can get this jeep started."

So we traded places. He pushed the starter button, and praise God, it started. He slowly turned the jeep around in the road and the Land Rover sput-sputtered the eight kilometers back to a doctor. No one panicked, and I was in no pain.

As we drove, the Spirit of the Lord came down on the jeep. We sang,

The Blood has never lost its Power.

When we got into the village, the jeep motor stopped and would not start again. By this time, the curfew was in effect, and the streets were empty. However, when the villagers saw our jeep, they came from behind their locked doors, like ants from the woodwork.

"Is there a doctor in this town?" Brother Hearn asked them.

"Yes! You have stopped right outside of his door."

So we went to the door and left the children in the jeep with Kathy. Although the doctor was asleep, he got up and invited us in.

I sat in his office, fully aware of all that went on around me, and still held the pillow over my eye. Marguerite was carried in and laid on the examination table. After he checked her feet, he came over to me and lifted the pillow from my face. I watched him go pale as he saw the extent of my injuries. My eyeball was on my cheek, and I was bleeding from four places. He scratched his nose, pulled his ear, and turned away. His body language was really encouraging! I knew I was going to die.

"I can't do anything for you. You'll have to go to Sagua La Grande," he told me.

Sagua la Grande was a town about thirty kilometers away. While we were in the office, a crowd formed outside. The doctor went out and announced, "We've got to get this party to Sagua La Grande. Is anyone willing to take them?"

Out of that crowd staggered an intoxicated man. "Yeah, I'll take them." When I heard about it, I wasn't sure he was the help we needed. He was a cab driver with an old '38 Chevrolet, who, because of the curfew, had decided to spend the night in town.

At the same time, a tall, distinguished gentleman stepped out of the crowd, and in English, told Kathy U'Ren, "I am a businessman in town, and I'd like to offer you hospitality. If some of you want to come to my home, I'll take care of you."

Kathy went to Milly. "Why don't I go with the children to this man's house?" Milly agreed, since she knew that Kathy was dependable, and the children felt secure with her.

We watched the Lord provide, Kathy told us later that as she and the children walked to the man's house, she thought that a warm cup of milk would be ideal to help the children to sleep. What did the gentleman's wife serve them? Mugs of hot milk.

The Hearns, Milly, and I got into the cab driver's car. He quickly had us on the road driving seventy miles per hour through the dark night. After all, he was an ambulance! I sat in the back and praised God. Hallelujah! We survived the ambush, but any second, this crazy character was going to roll the car, and we would all be with the Lord!

We arrived in Sagua la Grande at an antique Spanish mansion which had been converted into a hospital. When the cab driver came to a screeching hault in front of the building, I was told, "You just sit here. We'll go get help."

The Hearns, with Marguerite, went inside the hospital. I could see through the double entry doors a winding staircase. I watched as two Cuban orderlies struggled toward me with an empty stretcher. They laid it down and very ceremoniously indicated for me to get aboard. I asked, "Where are we going?"

They answered, "We've got to take you to the operating room, at the top of the marble stairs."

I volunteered, "I'll walk up."

"No, no! We've been detailed to carry you up."

I lay down on the stretcher. They had struggled when it was empty, but they really struggled with me on it! As we went up the staircase, they began to slip and slide. I thought, "I survived the ambush and the crazy cab driver, but any minute these orderlies are going to drop me over the side of the banister. I'll go to be with God!"

But they didn't drop me, and we made it to the operating room. They set the stretcher down.

After a short time the doctor came in and examined me. "We can't do anything for you here. You've got to go to Havana."

Havana was 250 miles from Sagua la Grande. There was no transportation available. There were no planes or trains. The roads were closed and bridges were burned. The doctor put a bandage over my eye and said, "We'll have to leave you as you are until the morning and then see what happens." He turned to examine Marguerite's feet.

All during the night, there were three of us in my room, my wife and I, and the Lord. I truly believed that I was going to die. I had no fear. The Bible tells us that "the grave has no victory, and death has no sting;" (1 Cor. 15:55) and just as I had preached it, I found it so. Any second I was going to be with the Lord!

In the midst of this joy, however, the devil taunted me. "Oh, so you're going to be with your Lord! That's great, but what about your wife and children?" All of a sudden the reality of my family's plight hit me. My wife, alone with five little children in a country in civil war and nowhere to go!

"Oh, God!" my soul cried out in agony. "Lord, Lord, how can I leave them at this time?"

Lord, How can I leave my precious ones at this time?

Then I heard the voice of the Lord, just as clear as can be, "Can't you trust them with me?"

The Spirit of the Lord in me said, "Of course I can! Of course!" I called out, "Oh, yes, Lord, of course! You could take better care of them than I ever could. I give them to Thee!" I expected to become unconscious and wake up with God. I even encouraged Him, "Well, Lord, I'm ready now. I'm ready to leave my wife and family with You and everything's going to be all right!"

But the voice of the Lord came back to me, "That's all I was waiting for. Now I'll tell you something else. Thou shalt not die, but live and declare the everlasting works of God!" (Psalm 118:17) Great joy and peace flooded my soul, and I fell asleep.

Some distance away, God spoke to another servant of His, an American Mennonite missionary named Adrian King. We had never heard of this man, and he certainly did not know us. God woke him in the middle of the night and said, "Get up. I want you to go out." He wondered where he should go. He had never heard from the Lord like that before. He wakened his wife and told her what he had heard. They tried to shrug it off and go back to sleep, but the voice was persistent.

"Darling? I . . . I . . . I think I must go out."

"Right now? In the middle of the night! Do you know what for?"

"No, I don't know why, but I'll have no peace until I go. I've got to go now." So he threw his bed cover back and looked at the clock. It was 3:00 A.M.

Mrs. King asked her husband, "Are you sure that it can't wait until morning?"

"I'm sure. Will you help me get ready?"

She got up, made him a sandwich, and something hot to drink.

"I think I'll take the station wagon," he mumbled as he finished dressing.

"But darling, you never take that car out unless we're going to the States for supplies. You always use the little Volkswagen."

"I just feel like taking the station wagon. Please put a mattress in the back of the wagon. I just might want to sleep on it; you never know." God sent him out without a map or set of directions. All that he had was the desire to obey. He drove around his town, then to the next town. He drove and drove. Two hours later, he arrived in Sagua La Grande. Tired of driving, he stopped outside of the town's hospital and wondered what to do next.

"Well, there's a hospital. I'll go and do a little visiting until I get further direction."

It was 5:00A.M. when he went up to the receptionist and asked, "I am a minister. I've just arrived in town and was wondering if I could visit the sick?"

"Of course," the receptionist answered. "Incidentally, there's a group of Americans, just like you, that came into town last night after an accident. You might want to stop and see them. They are upstairs." He knew immediately why the Lord had called him out.

The first thing Adrian said to us when he entered our room that morning was, "I'm at your service."

He was like an angel of God. "I have a station wagon with a mattress in the back. The injured can lie on it, and I can get through the back roads to Santa Clara." So he helped us all into his car, and we drove away.

We picked up the children and Kathy, then left the road. We traveled through rivers, sugar cane fields, and other rugged terrain. By 8:00 A.M., we entered Santa Clara.

We drove to the airport and found it shut down and surrounded by soldiers.

Milly volunteered, "Two weeks ago I met an American woman married to a Cuban doctor. She told me if we ever needed a doctor's help to go to them. At the time, I told her that we had lived in Cuba for five years and had not needed a physician, but she gave me directions to their apartment anyway. It is over by the town clinic."

So, with no other alternative, we drove to her apartment building. Milly knocked on their door. The doctor, who had just arrived home, came to the station wagon.

"Oh, my goodness!" he said to me, "you'll have to go to Havana!" Then he put his finger to his lip as if in thought, and said, "Wait a minute! There was a neurosurgeon from Havana, who came here a few days ago to see a special patient of his. He's been unable to fly back. He'd be the one. Now let me see. Where did he say he was staying?" He scratched his head and looked away from us. "If I can only remember where he said he was staying. . . . Well, there he is!" And there was the doctor from Havana walking across the street!

Our friend shouted the doctor's name, and he walked over to the station wagon.

Since he was a neurosurgeon, he looked at me and gave a very positive analysis. "There's nothing they can do for him in Havana that I can't do for him right here! Take him over to the clinic."

In the clinic, there was a simple little operating room and a few beds. I was still in no pain when they took me into the operating room. Milly was a fully trained nurse in England, so they allowed her to come in, too. As the doctor sorted through his tools, I noticed that he had a hammer, a chisel, a pair of pliers, and a little saw. They weren't common hardware tools, but they were clearly tools I could recognize. The three bullets that had plowed into my scalp were going to be removed with these tools!

I was not anesthetized, so I watched the doctor work on me. With the pliers he tried to grab the ends of the bullets, but the pliers slipped off of the tiny end of the bullet.

I wanted to say, "Hey, Doc, give me those pliers and let me do it!"

Finally, he wrenched one loose, but the others were too deeply imbedded. Next, he reached for his chisel and hammer. He chiseled off the top of the lodged bullets and sewed me up. Half way through this procedure, Milly walked out of the operating room; she couldn't handle any more.

Before I was taken out of the operating room, another doctor came and talked to the surgeon. A very kind, caring doctor told me, "I'm afraid we've got to have another little operation tomorrow."

The Lord had prepared my heart, so I said, "It's my eye, isn't it?"

"Yes, I'm afraid it is."

"Well, Doctor, you do whatever you feel you've got to do. We're trusting the Lord to show you what to do."

"Well, that's nice. Thank you."

I said, "We'll be praying for you."

"Thank you very much." And he left the room.

I was taken to my room, where Milly was allowed to stay on a little cot beside my bed. Still in no pain, I rejoiced in the presence of the Lord. "God is our refuge and strength, a very present help in trouble" (Psalm 46:1). I claimed that verse with all my heart that night.

An American government official in Santa Clara heard of the accident and came to the hospital to see if he could do anything for us. He sat in the room with us for four hours.

He couldn't believe we were alive! "Of the two hundred shots fired by the rebels, with eleven people in the jeep, only two of you were injured! There is a special feeling of God in this room, and He must have been with you in the ambush."

I slept on and off all that day and night. Nothing else could be done for me. However, the following morning, I was scheduled for the second operation.

Early the next morning, there was a knock on our door. Milly answered it and found a Cuban mother with three children offering to help us.

"Is there anything we can do for you? Do you need anything? Can we go out and buy anything for you? Do you need any messages delivered? Please, tell us. We want to help you."

Milly said, "Everything is being taken care of, thank you very much." We wondered after they left why they were so solicitous.

The doctor came in and said, "I took you at your word that I had freedom to do as I thought best. Your eyeball is intact, but your optic nerve is not. Another patient of mine needs a cornea. I have scheduled a transplant using your cornea. You have possibly seen the family of my patient. They are very grateful."

I turned to Milly. "Not even my eye will be wasted. Someone in Cuba will be able to see because of it!"

We were also concerned about Marguerite. Mr. Hearn came to see me. "Isn't our God faithful? Marguerite will be bed-ridden for many months, but she will be able to walk again. She even says she is grateful that she got hit by bullets in her feet, as she was running from the Lord, and the experience has brought her back to Him."

Ministers from almost every denomination came to our bedsides and prayed for us. Their love reaching out to us transcended the walls of doctrinal differences.

After only three days in the hospital, I was able to go home! Before releasing me, my doctor came into the room and sat by my bed. He picked up a little vial of antibiotic. "Marvelous! Fantastic!" he crooned.

I realized that he thought that it was that antibiotic that produced my speedy recovery. I didn't say that God didn't use the antibiotic, but I felt compelled to at least warn him, "Don't put too much confidence in that little bottle for the next patient, because it might not work as well. It was God who healed me!"

After the Ambush, 1959

P salm 46:1: "God is our refuge and strength, a very present help in trouble." We had read this verse, we had heard sermons on it, we had even quoted it, but all through the attack, we experienced it. God never left us, nor forsook us.

It amazed me that Ted had no bitterness toward the men who had attacked him. I, however, struggled with feelings of ill will. For example, while Ted was hospitalized, a visitor came to his room.

"I come with a message from Fidel Castro," he announced, "who wants you to know he's very sorry about what happened."

"Well, who are you?" I asked.

"I'm a Presbyterian minister."

"Well, you're in the wrong army, aren't you?" I asked impertinently, but honestly, as he turned red with embarrassment and changed the subject.

After he left, I asked Ted, "Darling, do you think the 'snakes' that were prophesied to surround and harm you were Fidel Castro's men in the ambush?"

"I will never think of those young men as snakes, Milly. They are precious souls that the Savior longs to bring to Himself."

"Should we leave Cuba?" I continued with my questions.

"Cuba is our home and our work is here. Where would we go?"

"The doctors here say that they can do nothing about the bullet still in your jaw. It's too near your facial nerve. They say that we need to get you to more experienced doctors in the United States," I replied.

"Well, the revolution is still on. There are soldiers on every road, and we could get shot again, if we went out on the streets. I think that for right now we should stay here. If the opportunity presents itself, we can consider leaving."

We received a telegram through the Red Cross: "Come Home. D&D Missionary Homes, St. Petersburg, Florida."

"Come home to Florida?" Ted asked in amazement. "We're British!"

The British government offered to get us out of Cuba, but we replied, "No, thank you. We're all right. We're biding our time and will get out as soon as God leads."

A couple of days later, we received another telegram from D&D Missionary Homes: "Come ye apart and rest awhile. Don't bring a thing. Everything is ready." As I read this short message to Ted, we both sat in wonderment. Who could these people be?

"Obviously, they're Christians and seem prepared to take care of us if we leave Cuba," I mused.

Ted was released from the clinic, and I put him to bed at home, glad for my years of nurse's training. Marguerite was also allowed to return home, and I spent a few minutes each day across the street with the Hearns. Marguerite's feet were improving daily.

One morning, Marguerite said, "You know, Milly, the ambush brought me back to Jesus." How true God's Word is: (Romans 8:28) "All things work together for our good. . . ." Peace flooded me, and I knew that it would work for us that way, too.

A week went by. Suddenly the rebels withdrew. The roads opened, and there was communication again to Havana. Ted and I agreed that we should take the opportunity to leave the country. We would accept the D&D hospitality, but what funds did we have to get us there?

Throughout our years as missionaries, the Lord had supplied what we needed as we needed it. However, the month before the accident, an unusual amount of money had come in from donors who never had sent money before. I remembered asking Ted, "What is this money for?"

"I don't know," he had replied, "but until it becomes clear, we'll just set it aside."

Again God had provided for our needs. After the ambush, we were able to pay the doctors, the hospitals, and still had enough to pay for our flight from Cuba.

"I don't know who the friendly people in Florida are, but we're soon going to find out," Ted said tiredly as our plane taxied to the runway at the Havana airport.

John Casteel, son of Richard Casteel, a fellow Cuban missionary, kindly drove our station wagon to Havana. He got our vehicle on a ferry, then met us in Miami with it. He drove us up to St. Petersburg to a big surprise. Two former Belgian Congo missionaries, Alma Doering and Stella Dunkleberger, both ninety-year-old "retired" missionaries, had set up several comfortable homes for missionaries to use when they needed a rest. (The "D&D" name was taken from the first letter of the last names of its cofounders.)

We recognized the frail and ailing Alma Doering as the same lady who had challenged us twenty-five years before to become missionaries. It amazed us to think that God had brought us full circle back to the same person who originally challenged us at the age of fourteen, with John 4:35, "Look on the fields; for they are ripe already to harvest."

I helped to care for Alma Doering until she went home to God in her sleep a few months later. We were blessed to sing at her funeral.

At this time, we could have gone across the country to speak, with a full schedule, since there were many people who wanted to hear Ted share his experiences. However, he couldn't open his mouth more than a half inch and was able to eat only soft foods. Loud noises disturbed him.

The D&D Missionary Homes personnel were true to their word and met our every need. One day, as I looked through the many boxes of donated food, I could not find two things that I wanted, honey and shortening. I needed the honey to make a hot drink for Ted, the shortening for Christmas cookies.

I feel sorry for those who don't believe in miracles. I've found God performs them quite regularly. As I was looking for the honey and shortening, a knock sounded at our door. When I opened it, there stood an old man with a pot of honey in one hand and a can of shortening in the other! He said, "I don't know why I brought these, but I'm Dr. Coopernale from New York, and I'd like to offer you my services." He became a wonderful friend and helped us in many ways.

Vic Graham, the minister from the church in Calgary, Canada, flew down to pray for my husband. After prayer, Ted's jaw released, and his mouth could move. How we re-

The Independent—

Cuban Missionary In Haven Here After Being Shot By Rebel Band

By NASH STUBLEN

Even a missionary preaching the word of God in Cuba knows the sting of bullets from the guns of the rebels of Fidel Castro.

Such a man is Edward Ware, 38, British missionary who, with his wife and five children, has been given a haven at the Missionary Rest Home of D & D Missions, Inc., just north of St. Petersburg.

His story began Sunday, Nov. 16, in Las Villas, the central provience in Cuba. Ware, whose black eye patch is a reminder of that day, said he and his family and four other missionaries were returning home to Santa Clara after a meeting in a small town about 35 miles away.

The Wares (she is a missionary also) had traveled many times the camp posts in the back country of Cuba where Castro's rebels hide out. "We always had complete freedom to preach the gospel without fear," he said.

Not so on this Sunday night as what sounded to some like a tire blowing out actually was a bullet being fired through the side of their vehicles. Ware realized that it was a gunshot and "I quickly turned on the car light to let them see who we were."

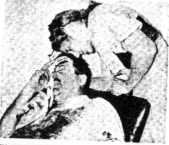

IN THIS PICTURE, snapped by a member of the Ware party, the wounded missionary is being comforted by his wife, immediately after the shooting. Ware himself bears no bitterness as a result of the event.

Recalling the words, "the Lord Jesus is with us everywhere," he added: "Such an experience enables us to see the words are actually his."

Ware observed:
"Only two were hit; we were able to limp into the next town and our vehicle stalled in front of the doctor's office."

It was 25 years ago that the Wares sat in a little church in London and became inspired enough by a woman missionary to decide to preach the gospel themselves.

The woman who inspired them is the same Mrs. Alma Doering, who is providing a haven for them now in a cottage in the 4000 block of Lealman avenue. Other missionaries — some sick and others just overworked — are being provided similar facilities.

The 80 - year - old missionary who retired from active work 10 years ago after 50 years service has since raised some $65,000 for investment in the cottages. She is being assisted now by Miss Louise Howard.

Meanwhile, the Wares said they expect to remain here until the road is clear again for them to carry on their work. Ware, who served in the Royal Air Force in World War II, and his family are taking heed to the words that are inscribed on the sign in front of the cottages:

"Come Ye Apart and Rest Awhile."

joiced! Later, when we went to get Ted an American driver's license, we learned that the sight in his remaining eye had improved to 20/20!

We then needed to decide whether Ted ought to have surgery to remove the lodged bullet in his jawbone. The risks were high, since the facial nerve was very close to where the doctors would have to remove the bullet. After prayer and discussion, since Ted had no pain and full range of movement in his jaw, we decided to leave the bullet where it was. For forty years the bullet has lodged in his jawbone with no discomfort. However, it is still there! It can be seen in X-rays.

A lady from Canada wrote to us while we were in St. Petersburg. She informed us that on the night of the ambush, after returning from church, at the precise time we were being shot, she had gone to her well for water.

"To my surprise," she wrote, "when I stopped pumping the well, I started speaking in tongues. I found myself interceding for the life of Ted Ware. I stayed there until I got freedom in my heart to stop."

Another woman, a schoolteacher in Seattle, wrote us at our Cuban address. The letter was forwarded and reached us some time later. "What happened to you in November? God has filled my heart with a love for you that has kept me praying for you daily."

There were many others. From all over the world and from many denominations, we learned we had been prayed for, not only at the time of the ambush, but faithfully over the years. To them we say, "You sowed, and we reaped, but we both rejoice in the fruit of His hand."

Epilogue

On June 5, 1999, at the age of seventy-eight, Ted, in his sleep, went to be with the Lord. A few weeks before, he shared with his family a vivid dream that he had had. He saw himself at a river. On the far side, there was a beautiful grassy knoll that he described as having the most beautiful green grass that he had ever seen. Growing in the grass were trees. Leaning up against one tree was his best friend, Dick Cochrane, who had died numerous years before. He stood there with his arms folded in front, smiling at him, as if he were waiting for him. Leaning up against another tree was Paul Gifford, one of Ted's close friends from Canadian boot camp days. In the early 1950's, Paul had died fighting a fire at the camp in California. Ted recalled his being sent from Canada to California to identify Paul's remains and to then inform Paul's parents. In the dream, Ted saw his friends well and happily waiting for him.

It would take another book to tell of the years between 1959 and 1999. Concluding this book, I would like to share a statement by Lyle Herbaugh from "Celebrating the Home-going of Pastor Edward P. Ware." This excerpt from a church newsletter, *Glad Tidings*, July 1999, an official publication of the Avon United Methodist Church of Mt. Vernon, Washington, follows:

On June 9th we celebrated the life of Pastor Edward Ware. It was the most inspiring memorial I have ever attended. This was a celebration of love: love for the Lord, love for his wife, love for his family. The room was filled with love. This was a celebration of serving, serving the Lord in ways most of us can not imagine. This was a celebration of inspiration; for this man, through his love and his service, inspired many people to stand firm in their belief in God and to go out and serve the Lord.

Posted in the church parlor was a map of the world studded with colored pins; red ones for the missions Pastor Ware had started, or in which he had served; white flags for the churches he had started. The pins were everywhere, scattered across several continents. Standing there in front of the map, it became clear to me that One man can make a difference. I was inspired to love the Lord with all my heart and to follow His call.

WITH A LOVE

Ted Ware

Adap. from Old German Aire

To order additional copies of

WITH
A
LOVE

Have your credit card ready and call

(877) 421-READ (7323)

or send $12.95 each plus $3.95* S&H to

WinePress Publishing
PO Box 428
Enumclaw, WA 98022

* add $1.00 S&H for each additional book ordered